THE

Naturalista

To Ben:

The mortar to my pestle,

and the undisputed king of cornershop dahl.

THE

Naturalista

NOURISHING RECIPES TO LIVE WELL
XOCHI BALFOUR

PHOTOGRAPHY BY RAHEL WEISS

headline

CONTENTS

THE NATURALISTA WAY
NOURISHING RECIPES TO LIVE WELL

I write a natural living and wellness blog called The Naturalista (www.thenaturalista.co.uk), which explores holistic health in all its many forms. I am passionate about living a balanced, natural life in harmony with the world around us and believe that the three pillars of optimal health and vitality are a wholefood diet, natural skincare and the cultivation of mindfulness. I am currently finishing my training as a naturopathic nutritionist, the principles of which inform this book: nourishing inside and out with natural ingredients. All my recipes are gluten- and dairy-free and are largely plant-based – although some do contain meat and fish, which many of us need from time to time. I also think we should be eating fresh ingredients in their natural state as much as we can, so many dishes are entirely raw.

MY WELLNESS JOURNEY

In 2011, I quit my office job in London with my (now) husband Ben to set up a charitable healthy street food truck, called Rainbo. We were not chefs – although Ben was an enthusiastic and accomplished cook and we spent most of our evenings devouring every page of Ottolenghi's *Plenty* – and we had limited street food experience, knife skills or knowledge of what would be involved. But we knew we needed to do it, to hit the road and follow our dreams. We restored an old 1948 Ford pickup, concocted a healthy lunchtime box of homemade gyoza dumplings and rainbow salad and roamed the streets to sell it. The adventure was a wild and wonderful blur of chopping, griddling, washing, packing, driving, eating, laughing and sharing (and occasional crying) and after a year or so running the van I hit what I now see was adrenal burnout. Back-to-back days of stressful trading, getting home at 2am and up to prep at 6, scoffing whatever was around us for fuel – usually burgers, hotdogs, brownies and coffee – had left me exhausted, depleted and running on empty with my heart thumping in my throat. The culmination of this, amid stubborn tears of exhaustion and an almost total abandonment of my social life or any family time, was having a panic attack on my bedroom floor late one night while too tired to fall asleep. And although the street food lifestyle is an extremely demanding one, I know I am not the only one to feel like their life is suddenly in control of them and not the other way round. Longer work hours, crowded commutes, eating on the run and the round-the-clock demands of life lived online all creep in upon us and keep stress levels running impossibly high. I knew that if we were to continue giving our business our all – or anything at all – something major had to shift.

What we put into our mouths struck me as the most important place to start. Burgers, fried chicken and all sorts of refined sugar treats may make for a great street food night out but they are not what we were designed to live on. I enrolled in a short course on nutrition at the College of Naturopathic Medicine and it was like a spark had been lit inside me: I needed to learn how the fuel we feed our bodies works, and all the things I could do to get myself back on track. I needed to reclaim my power. Not since my days at Oxford had I known such a thirst for learning, and I immediately enrolled in the three-year Naturopathic Nutrition diploma. Following swiftly on from overhauling our diet and kitchen cupboards, the bathroom cabinet came next, alongside a chance journey to a silent retreat and meditation community in Costa Rica. A more conscious and mindful approach to living took seed and continues to flourish as I discover more and more about healing foods, natural skincare and the path of self enquiry – and how they intertwine.

Looking around me, I know I'm not the only one to go through this, and it is an honour and a passion to share what I have discovered so far about staying 'well' in the whirlwind of modern life. This book is a simple, inspiring wellness bible for anyone who needs to slow down, listen to their bodies and get themselves back on track. You don't need to take a week off work and trek to a meditation retreat or do a costly juice cleanse; you don't need to spend a fortune on expensive treatments or therapies: the ingredients you need to live a healthier, happier life are right here. I changed my whole life from my little London kitchen and had tremendous fun doing it; this book is the culmination of what I have learned.

HOW I LIVE AND EAT NOW

Regardless of what healthy eating fads may grace the press and your social media feed, the best judge of how you should eat is yourself. Our bodies have an innate wisdom and if we learn to listen to them properly, we start to eat what we need, and ditch the things we do not. In my twenties, I was vegetarian for four years and while I felt wonderful morally speaking, I felt terrible physically. My immune system was weak, my diet was poor, and cheese and carbs were the mainstay of my meals. I now know a great deal more about how to live a healthy meat-free life, but I have discovered through trial and error that I feel at my best when I incorporate meat, fish and eggs into my diet; particularly because as a female with a strong monthly cycle, my body gives me very clear signals when it wants red meat – and no popular diet or health food craze can compete with vividly dreaming about steak.

My food philosophy follows the main naturopathic principles, and this also applies to what I put on my skin: nothing processed, gluten free, predominantly plant-based with plenty of healthy fats, organic and Fairtrade wherever possible. I avoid gluten and dairy because my husband is intolerant to them and his digestive and immune systems flare up when he eats them. He is one of a growing number, and the body's inflammatory response to both ingredients is an obstacle on the road to good health for many of us.

Furthermore, the ways in which much dairy is farmed these days, from poor animal welfare to antibiotics, genetically modified feed and hormone use, is almost unrecognisable from the raw, natural, unpasteurised milk that previous generations enjoyed. For this reason I prefer to avoid it on the whole. I eat meat three or four times a month and fish more or less once a week. I follow the SMASH acronym for cold-water, Omega-3-rich and responsibly sourced wild fish (from large to small): salmon, mackerel, anchovies, sardines and herring. The recipes in this book cater for raw, vegetarian and vegan lifestyles as well, and are labelled accordingly so you can easily identify them.

Plant foods, leafy greens and fibrous vegetables are vital for optimal health and disease prevention and often acutely lacking in the modern western diet. The dominance of processed meats, dairy, sugars, additives and preservatives leads to all sorts of imbalance and disease, most increasingly in the colon where increased transit time and lack of fibre to move things through properly contributes to rising numbers of IBS diagnoses and other health complaints. With this in mind, I encourage everyone to eat as many plants as they can each day; ideally the plate should be two-thirds fruit or vegetables. Once we start to increase our fibre we usually notice dramatic differences in bowel elimination, complexion, energy and vitality.

In a world where processed food abounds, I try to make as much as I can from scratch as it is the only way to have complete control over what I am putting in my body. However, I know how busy we all are, and there are now some fantastic ready-made products available that bring us the best of nourishing wholefoods in a convenient and affordable way, helping us make the shift to a healthier way of eating quickly and easily. Dairy-free milks, nut butters and vanilla bean paste are three examples of ready-made health food ingredients that I always make sure I have well stocked. Just be sure to opt for the unsweetened milks where you can, and those without any hidden or unnecessary ingredients (for more on this see pages 20–31). In my experience, it's better to change any lifestyle or eating habits gradually and in a sustainable way that works for you in the long term – perhaps by swapping your usual peanut butter for almond butter, or by experimenting with a new ingredient, like coconut oil – as this means those changes are more likely to stick, and the benefits to really take root. (This also applies to skincare: in my mind the nutrients, ingredients and harmful chemicals to avoid are not dissimilar whether we are thinking about the foods we eat or the products we use on our skin.)

In everything, balance is the key to health and happiness. Feeling restricted and deprived does no one any good and I don't see anything criminal about enjoying wine, coffee and other treats in moderation if you consciously support your body around them.

NATURAL BEAUTY: RECLAIM YOUR POWER

For me, adopting a more natural approach to skincare and what we put on our body's largest organ is a natural extension of choosing to eat more healthily. In the whirlwind age we live in, where stress and disease levels are permanently on the rise, and we find ourselves constantly consuming under the influence of multinational corporations, consciously returning to a natural way of living, in harmony with the planet, is one of the most empowering things we can do. And nowhere is this more pressing than in the skincare sphere.

Parabens, sodium laureth sulfate (a foaming agent) and an ever-growing army of chemically manufactured preservatives, thickeners, colourants, fragrances and fillers are packed into so many of the everyday beauty products

we buy, from deodorant and toothpaste to body scrubs and lotions. Until only recently we assumed they must be good for us. And while research on the potential dangers of these is growing, and laws are tightening in areas to reflect this, as consumers we need to keep our eyes wide open and consciously foster a healthy curiosity about what exactly we are putting on our skin. It is just as important as what we eat, if not more so, for the sole reason that throughout the day, week and year we vary our diet and eating habits, yet we tend to loyally clutch on to one chemical-filled toothpaste, shaving cream and deodorant and use it once or twice a day for years on end.

Through developing my own little natural army of everyday beauty essentials, I have not only cultivated a sense of empowerment as I learn new skills and recipes, but also a growing appreciation for my body – my hard-working apparatus – and the wealth of healing ingredients that can nourish it. Some things, like shampoo and conditioner, I leave to the scientists to get right: there are so many brilliant natural beauty lines emerging and what we cannot make ourselves can be sourced consciously and responsibly from a growing number of brands. But what we can make becomes part of our wellness journey, and just as with food, through trial and error we can make it our own – it is one of the most exciting things to undertake.

LIVING MORE MINDFULLY

For me, living more mindfully, with more awareness in all that we say and do, is the absolute cornerstone of achieving optimum vitality. Meditation, self-enquiry and learning to look inside and sit with what we find there – not outrunning it with busyness or mindless consuming – are the foundations for living a balanced life where mind and body coexist in harmony. Our emotional state has such a profound and direct impact on our physiology and if we are stressed, worried or distracted by the workings of the mind it is not only our mood that is affected: our digestion, hormones, blood sugar, bowels, skin and so much more can begin to fall into disarray as well. For me, this fundamental link between body and mind is at the core of vitality (literally, our life force).

Throughout my Naturalista journey I have travelled to teachers and workshops near and far to explore the many wonderful ways in which we can dive inside and better know ourselves. It isn't always easy facing our true selves and all the negative emotions that we so often hide, but the rewards are the key to balance and wellness.

I know from living in the confines of London and the frenzy of everyday life that it is not always easy to find time each day to meditate alone. But even closing my eyes, connecting to my breath and observing the mind for five minutes a day can dramatically transform the way I approach my daily life and how I relate to myself and others. Meditation also helps us get to know ourselves on a profound level; in this meeting with the whole self we are able to explore and purge stagnant emotion and energy that no kale, green juice or workout can expel. We find anger, joy, passion, jealousy, sadness… the whole rainbow of human emotions that can be so easily repressed in everyday life, populating our internal landscape. Without acknowledgement, they can all too easily begin to block our energy, our chakras, our life force from flowing freely. Trapped emotions manifest as physical imbalances and vitality hits a short circuit.

In the third section of this book, you will find simple everyday tools and tips that harness techniques from the many traditions I have learned from – be it yogic, naturopathic, shamanic or what generally falls under the 'spiritual' umbrella – and that keep me grounded and connected to my truth in the humdrum of modern life. You don't have to renounce all your possessions and run off into the forest (although this would probably be a very liberating move!). Just as a small switch to eating more veggies or making your own face scrub opens the door to greater changes, so a gentle daily or weekly meditation can have a profound effect on all that you do. You just have to jump in and see; you might be surprised at the goodness you find there.

PANTRY

A well-stocked pantry is key to stress-free nutritional cooking and while it may seem like a big commitment at first, once you invest in a few star ingredients, you will find it so much easier to improvise with what you have in the kitchen, and grow your own unique repertoire of go-to wholefood recipes. A little nut butter, cacao and bee pollen can turn the dreariest smoothie into a delicious nutrient-packed breakfast; a handful of brown rice or quinoa with some tamari seeds or nori can jazz up almost any leftover veggies. With an army of staples to hand you can start to improvise with ingredients, minimise waste and really become rooted in healthy cooking in your own way – beyond just following recipes and throwing out the leftovers. This list covers the basics and is a great place to start but I really encourage you to keep exploring the shop aisles and find your own beloved staples to go alongside them.

PLANTS VERSUS ANIMALS

As I said in the introduction, I believe that the optimal diet is largely plant-based, with occasional animal protein coming from eggs, meat and fish (preferably oily cold-water fish, see below).

Eggs are a dense source of nutrients and protein and are brilliantly versatile; having a good store of organic, free-range ones means you are never short of a good base for an emergency omelette, frittata, or healthy bowl (see Salmon, Kale and Egg Bowl, page 54) to keep hunger pangs at bay. I eat meat and fish occasionally because I feel better when I do; it is always good to buy organic, sustainable meat and fish from a reliable source, and in my view it is preferable to have a good-quality cut once a fortnight or so, than a cheap one every other day. If you subscribe to an organic box, many suppliers also offer meat and this is a great way to make sure you get a variety of good-quality, ethically reared options. If you lead a very busy life it is also helpful to freeze cuts or mince to have in store for when you feel you need it.

When buying fish, I tend to follow the cold-water SMASH acronym (salmon, mackerel, anchovies, sardines and herring) as these are rich in Omega-3, and I always buy sustainably sourced, and wild where possible. This mostly applies to salmon, where a bright red colour indicates to me a rich supply of oxygen and denser nutrient content. Nutritionally speaking, unsmoked fish and meat are preferable over smoked, but a little deviation from this rule every now and then should not be too frowned upon: if it is from a good source, it is good protein, so go for it.

Because my husband is intolerant to both, along with an increasing number of us following the western diet, I opt not to cook with dairy or gluten, which can provoke an inflammatory response and put a strain on many of the body's processes and systems (see the Introduction for more on this). Regardless of this, in these days of antibiotic-laden dairy farming I feel increasingly wary of cow's milk and always make or buy nut, seed or coconut milk instead. Most of the time I make my own (see page 164) but you do need a Vitamix or high-performance blender. If you don't have one (or don't have time), the shop-bought options are getting better and better, covering many types of nuts and seeds – just opt for minimal sugar, additives and heat processing. If you know you will be busy, it is a good idea to stock up on a few cartons to have on hand for breakfasts and hot drinks. (They can usually be kept at room temperature so check the packaging.)

It is more difficult to obtain all the nutrients we need from a strictly plant-based diet – but by no means impossible. For those following a vegetarian or vegan diet, I have created recipes with the essential nutrients – and their denser superfood sources – in mind, to provide as balanced and nutritionally 'complete' a menu as possible. I also support the use of prescribed nutritional supplements when necessary to make sure vegans and vegetarians meet their optimal macro- and micronutrient requirements. There are plenty of reputable plant-based supplement companies whose ranges are designed to support vegan and vegetarian diets, and they can be a great help alongside your daily food intake.

BUDGET

The central tenet of my cooking, and of this book, is wholefoods above all else. This doesn't have to mean nothing but costly powders and rare brands of free-from nut milk – instead it encourages a return to cooking with whole, unprocessed foods, as plant-based and unrefined as possible, as an everyday foundation from which to live well. I didn't forge a nutritional path with a bulging wallet and don't expect others to: what superfoods I can afford, I invest in, because their benefits are highly valuable in a busy modern life. But at the heart of my food and beauty recipes lies an emphasis on fresh, accessible ingredients that won't break the bank. Everyday foods such as lentils and dark leafy greens contain a vast array of essential vitamins and minerals themselves – the powders and sprinkles add further micronutrients and can be added or left out as you wish. The exception is perhaps nut butter (almond or cashew), which costs a little more than peanut butter but is much healthier. It has become invaluable to me, particularly where breakfasts and smoothies are concerned; I buy it in bulk to keep costs down and devour it with almost anything.

BALANCED CONSUMER CHOICES

With a cultivation of more mindful living and healthier cooking comes a natural heightening of environmental awareness. The materials we use and buy, the clothes we wear, the supply chains of the products and companies we support all come into question: every time we make a purchase we express support of one code of ethics or another. However, I believe that everything is a compromise and that in holistic health terms, the best can sometimes be the enemy of the good. The way I see it, if you make the switch to eat more organic veg but only buy them from your local supermarket, it is better than eating none at all; if you start to drink more water but it comes in a plastic bottle, don't beat yourself up – the move is a good one and the BPA-free bottle can come later (see Storage, page 31). No one is perfect and we are constantly refining our choices as we evolve. Through these evolving values we change our habits, not with an extreme all-or-nothing zeal, but a progressive awareness of how we would like to, and are able to, live our lives.

ORGANIC VERSUS
NON-ORGANIC

If we are to absorb and utilise the optimal amount of nutrients from the ingredients we eat and put on our skin, the ideal choice is always to buy organic. Aside from the absence of potentially harmful pesticides and chemicals, organic produce is grown in mineral-rich soil and thus contains a higher density of micronutrients. Furthermore, without the commercial mollycoddling that industrial farming has recourse to, the plants grow stronger and more nutrient-dense as they strengthen their defences against predators and the environment. Nowhere is this more apparent than in the flavour of a seasonal tomato or cucumber grown in organic soil – the comparison with their non-organic equivalent speaks volumes.

There are a number of good weekly veg box schemes emerging throughout the UK and this is a great way to not only ensure a full fridge but also of supporting local farming and trade. You will also invariably have to cook an unexpected vegetable at some point and this bottom-of-the-box moment is when some of my most interesting recipes have sprung to life.

MY GO-TO
INGREDIENTS

GRAINS
There are plenty of gluten-free grains to choose from in most shops and having a good supply in the cupboard means you are never short of a quick and easy accompaniment to salads and veggies. Quinoa, technically a seed but known as the sacred grain of the Incas, contains all the amino acids (the building blocks for protein) that cannot be produced by the body, making it a complete protein option for plant-based diets. It is also high in calcium, iron, B vitamins and vitamin E. You can buy white, black and red varieties – always make sure to choose Fairtrade, and organic where possible. You should also rinse it before cooking, as it is coated with compounds called saponins, which can give it a soapy taste. Buckwheat, which is a fruit seed related to rhubarb and sorrel, is also high in protein and a flavanoid (a family of phytochemicals) called rutin, which supports cardiovascular health, can help enhance the action of vitamin C and provide antioxidant and anti-inflammatory benefits. You can buy it loose in groat form (as a hulled kernel), as a flour or as quick-and-easy soba noodles. Whole brown, black and red rice are also versatile gluten-free grains that are widely available and won't break the bank.

Beyond the recipes that involve them, grains are a quick and easy addition to any meal: boiled in a little stock (see page 178), they take in tons of flavour and dressed with some oil, tamari, fresh herbs and toasted seeds they have become a staple add-on to any dish or meal in our kitchen. Black and red rice and quinoa are a particularly easy way to bring some colour and substance to a plate with minimal planning or prep. Some gently toasted buckwheat is also a lovely crunchy topping on salads or roast veggies.

I occasionally like to use oats as they are also affordable, accessible and naturally gluten-free: it is only in contact with other grains that they may become contaminated with gluten. They are a rich source of silicon (vital for bone and connective tissue health) and phosphorous (needed for brain and nerve formation).

FLOUR

One of the joys of owning a Vitamix is that it can pulverise almost any grain into a fine flour; however gluten-free flours can also be bought from most health food stores if you do not have one. I try to avoid obscure flours in my recipes for the simple reason that they tend to cost more and are harder to source. However, buckwheat flour binds and adds a lovely nutty flavour to the Beetroot Falafel (see page 110) and ground oats are a vital component of my Everyday Courgette Bread (see page 162).

NUTRITIONAL YEAST

I use nutritional yeast for cheesy flavour – it can be sprinkled on almost anything in an emergency. It is made from a yeast called *saccharomyces serevisiae*, which is dried at high temperatures to deactivate it. It comes in flakes, which have a deliciously more-ish savoury flavour. Once you try it, it can be hard to leave the pot alone… They don't call it vegan crack for nothing.

NUTS AND SEEDS

Whether lightly toasted, blended for milk (see page 164), sliced, crushed or simply eaten raw as a snack, nuts and seeds are wonderfully versatile ingredients and always in abundance in our kitchen. They are a good source of protein, fibre and essential fatty acids: alpha-linolenic acid (Omega-3) and linoleic acid (Omega-6), fats that we need in the body but cannot make ourselves and must obtain through food. Each type has its own unique nutrient profile: seeds such as pumpkin (especially high in magnesium and zinc), sesame and sunflower are good protein sources for those with nut intolerances. Chia seeds are a rich source of fibre (and Omega-3) and make a great healthy snack soaked in some milk and topped with fruit. Flaxseed (which comes in brown or yellow) is one of the densest plant-based sources of Omega-3 and is a great way for vegans to get their required intake. Almonds make delicious milk and are a good source of calcium; cashews and macadamias are good for creamy sweet dishes, although they are a little richer and can sometimes cause digestive disruption if consumed in excess, so are best eaten in moderation; Brazil nuts contain high levels of the essential mineral selenium, which plays an important role in thyroid and immune function (two or three a day are sufficient to meet the recommended intake); walnuts are particularly high in antioxidants and Omega-3 fatty acids, which provide anti-inflammatory and brain health benefits (perhaps no coincidence that they are shaped like one). All nuts (except cashews which are technically seeds) should ideally be soaked for at least six or seven hours before use to reduce the phytic acid, tannins and enzyme inhibitors present in their outer layers (which can interfere with vitamin and mineral absorption), increase their vitamin and enzyme content and make them easier to digest.

It's always better to buy raw nuts and then toast them yourself; choose organic if you can, especially with cashews as these are often bleached to look whiter than they are. Store all nuts in airtight containers and out of direct sunlight.

OILS

There is so much debate over which oils are best to cook with and new research constantly touts this one as 'dangerous' and that one as 'healthy'. I think the main questions to consider are volatility, purpose, flavour and price. If you eat predominantly raw food, oils will provide the bulk of your fats, and omega-rich ones such as cold-pressed hemp, flax and olive are a good option. Flax should be kept in the dark in the fridge; the other two are more stable at room temperature. For cooking, the higher the smoke point (the temperature at which the oil undergoes molecular transformation and begins to break down) the better. Avocado oil and coconut oil have very high smoke points, olive oil can also withstand relatively high heat and I tend to cook mostly with the latter two, as recommended throughout this book, because they are good value and easy to come by. (Coconut oil is also an amazingly versatile natural beauty ingredient and I keep a pot in the bathroom too – see page 206 for more about its natural beauty uses.) From a nutritional point of view it is always preferable to keep frying to a minimum, and I try to stick to this rule in my recipes. For salads and to use at lower temperatures, a mix of nutty hemp and traditional olive oil is my favourite but play around and find your preferred blends. Always opt for cold-pressed and organic oils.

SALT

As with sugar, salt is needed in the body in small amounts but should be eaten in moderation. I cook with pink Himalayan salt, which contains an abundance of minerals and has a sweet, well-rounded flavour. Grey or black salt is also a good option; anything bright white – even if labelled sea salt – has almost always undergone some sort of refining and/or bleaching process and been stripped of some if not all of its micronutrients. Everyday table salt is also usually mixed with chemical anti-caking agents (often containing aluminium) and is best avoided. When cooking it is a good idea to vary your sources of saltiness, for both taste and good health. Tamari (gluten-free soy sauce), miso paste and soaked sundried tomatoes (or their water) are great alternatives to salt and provide a rich depth of flavour. Tamari can vary quite dramatically in concentration so always start cautiously and taste as you go.

SPICES

I was always rather apprehensive of using spices until I moved in with Ben and discovered a lifetime's supply of cumin, cardamom, cinnamon, sumac, turmeric, saffron, fennel and coriander seeds. He showed me how to use them in everyday cooking and the wonderfully uplifting and transformative effects they can have on grains, veggies and stews with little cost and effort. Many are powerful medicinal kitchen aids and my favourites are cinnamon, turmeric and ginger (see more on these in my Food Heroes pages 44, 71 and 133). I also love saffron and cardamom for their take-me-travelling aromas and distinctive flavour (I often use cardamom in natural body scrubs too for some uplifting bath time aromatherapy, see page 238). Store your spices out of direct sunlight, and if you find some older ones in your cupboard you can quickly revive them in a dry frying pan over a low heat for 30 seconds.

SUGARS

Throughout this book I alternate honey, maple syrup and coconut palm sugar as my main sources of sweetness. I do not believe that one is dramatically healthier than another; all sugars are unhealthy if consumed in excess and my aim when cooking is to use the least refined, most naturally occurring options that maximise on flavour, and use them sparingly. In most recipes I encourage you to sweeten according to your own taste, and the ideal should always be as little as possible; even if you have a very sweet tooth you can very gradually lessen the amount of added sugar as you go. Unrefined coconut palm sugar comes from the blossom of the coconut palm flower and has a delicious butterscotchy flavour; it has a similar taste to brown sugar but a lower glycaemic index (meaning it doesn't cause such a dramatic spike in blood glucose levels). Maple syrup should always be pure – watch out for the diluted versions, which are bulked up with carob syrup. Honey (for non-vegans) is best bought raw, unprocessed and – if possible – local. As with coconut oil, I use this frequently for natural beauty recipes as well (see pages 212–213 for more information on its healing properties). Manuka honey, from New Zealand and Australia, is a more expensive option and popular for its rich flavour and increased level of an immunity-boosting antibacterial compound called methyglyoxal. This antimicrobial activity is measured by a UMF (Unique Manuka Factor) – anything over 10 means the honey is 'active' and suitable for therapeutic medical use. The lowest UMF is 0 and the highest is 16+ and the level is usually reflected in the price.

SUPERFOODS

Throughout my nutritional journey I have always incorporated superfoods wherever I can. By superfoods, I mean foods that contain a particularly high concentration of beneficial phytonutrients, the compounds found in plants that help prevent disease and maintain optimal health and vitality. Plenty abound, from blueberries to maca; some are cheap while others are more expensive. Variety is key in healthy cooking and eating; I try to mix them up as much as possible and incorporate them into my recipes as optional extras as opposed to the main focal point. Here are my favourites from health food stores and online; where possible, always buy from a sustainable and organic source:

ACAI: This dark purple Brazilian fruit is high in antioxidant pigments called anthocyanins: it has one of the highest ORAC (Oxygen Radical Absorbance Capacity) counts of any fruit or vegetable and as such is very effective at mopping up harmful free radicals. It has a tart flavour similar to berries and chocolate and its rich colour makes it a great addition to puddings and smoothies (see also the Raw Acai and Blueberry 'Cheesecake' on page 140). You can buy the berries in frozen or powdered form from most health food stores.

BEE POLLEN: This is the pollen from flowers that gathers on the legs of worker bees. It is packed with vitamins, minerals and proteins and as such is often referred to as a 'complete superfood'. About 50% of its protein is present as free amino acids that are ready to be assimilated by the body, and it has been shown to reduce the presence of histamine, involved in the allergic response. Although it is delicious and intensely more-ish, it should be used sparingly as a treat: it takes a very long time for the bees to make and we do not need enormous spoonfuls every day. Always makes sure you buy bee pollen from a sustainable source and store it in an airtight pouch or container.

Cacao: Unprocessed cacao contains high amounts of beneficial phytonutrients and is a rich source of magnesium and antioxidants. Added to smoothies and sweet treats, it boosts energy levels and releases a compound called anandamide, which creates a feeling of open-heartedness, excitement and more energy. Raw cacao, extracted from the beans by cold-pressing them to remove the fat without killing their living enzymes, is different from its processed cousin cocoa, which is extracted at high temperatures and is stripped of many of its nutrients, if not all. Cacao nibs are the solid version, which are ground for powder. Both are great to have in the pantry and cacao nibs make a good snack with some goji berries and pumpkin seeds.

Maca: The Incan warrior's natural fuel and often referred to as Peruvian ginseng, maca root is a powerful adaptogen (a plant that can support the body's response to stress), rich in plant sterols that help increase stamina and fight fatigue. It supports the thyroid and adrenals and helps to regulate metabolism and hormone production. The powdered root has a malty, semi-sweet taste and is a great addition to breakfasts and smoothies when a natural boost in energy is needed. Ashwaganda powder is also a highly beneficial adaptogen for adrenal fatigue and can be used in the same way.

Seaweed: Sea plants can contain from 10–20 times the minerals of land plants and are becoming an increasingly available nutritional kitchen supplement. All are rich sources of calcium, iodine and iron. Nori has the highest protein content of all the seaweeds (almost 50% when dry) and is a good source of vitamins A, B1 and minerals niacin and iodine – vital for thyroid function and metabolic health. My Nori Za'atar Sprinkle (see page 175) is an absolute saviour in our busy household, and often I will serve a dip or dahl with a sheet of nori on the side for extra plant-based goodness and protein. Arame (very high in iodine) and wakame (very high in calcium) can also be used in its place or as an addition to salads and raw dishes; all come dried and can be easily stored, soaked or eaten as they are. Make sure you buy organic seaweed and always opt for a brand that has a clear policy regarding radiation and heavy metal testing.

Spirulina: The algae spirulina consists of over 60% protein and contains all the essential amino acids that we need and cannot make ourselves. It is rich in readily available iron (as well as an abundance of other minerals and B vitamins) and its bright pigment, phycocyanin, is known for its antioxidant and anti-inflammatory effects. It is worth noting that while spirulina is often praised for containing high amounts of vitamin B12 (at risk of deficiency in vegan diets) the B12 occurs in an inactive form in

PANTRY

the plant (known as 'analogue') and it is not recommended as a reliable source of the nutrient. A little goes a long way and spirulina is best consumed in small amounts: excessive daily intake may mean that its beneficial action of binding on to and eliminating heavy metals from the blood (known as chelation) may work the other way and rid our blood of vital minerals. I use a heaped teaspoon of spirulina once or twice a week.

Wheatgrass: Wheatgrass powder is a rich, plant-based source of vitamins A, C and all the B vitamins, as well as magnesium, iron, calcium and amino acids. It is abundant in a beneficial phytonutrient called apigenin (also found in alfalfa and parsley), believed to have strong antioxidant effects, and it is also a dense source of chlorophyll, thought to help cleanse blood and protect against carcinogens. It's particularly helpful in the city, where we are exposed to so many pollutants from traffic fumes. The powder form is widely available online and in stores and has a much milder taste than the juice.

EQUIPMENT

I try to use the least obscure or expensive kitchen equipment when cooking and making natural beauty products; in most cases you can use your regular kitchen equipment and often for beauty recipes all you need is a spoon and a couple of bowls. Here are some things that I consider essential in any healthy kitchen:

VITAMIX
The exception to the above rule is my Vitamix, which blends almost anything at incredibly high speed and which has been instrumental in my transition to healthy cooking. I recommend saving up for one to anyone; however the blender world is getting brilliantly competitive and there are plenty of cheaper options that will be just fine for everyday smoothies, soups and puddings.

NUT MILK BAG
I rely heavily on one of these to make my Nut Milk (see page 164) but a muslin cloth will do just fine.

SPIRALISER
This increasingly popular kitchen gadget is used to make vegetable 'spaghetti' (see page 109), a fun way to replace refined wheat pasta. They are relatively cheap to buy but you can also use a julienne peeler, which is smaller and less expensive.

KNIVES
I have a good set of professional knives and learning to use these properly (with plenty of scrapes along the way) has made all the difference when slicing and dicing. A good chopping knife, paring knife and filleting knife are my three essentials. If you're not a seasoned chopper a mezzaluna is brilliant for herbs, and quite fun to use so it will encourage you to throw as many as you can into your meals; in my opinion, the more the merrier almost always applies.

GRATER, PEELER AND MANDOLINE

I recommend using good-quality graters and peelers, while a mandoline is perfect if you are not confident with very fine slicing. But use these with care as they are often razor sharp. They allow you to make quick work of slicing and keep things nice and consistent.

INFUSION TEAPOT

I make herbal tea blends in our infusion teapot, but you can also use a regular cafetière.

MUFFIN TRAY

I use an enamel muffin tray to cook muffins and also for my natural Shea Body Lotion Bars (see page 200) – it requires thorough washing up afterwards to get rid of the essential oils (Ecover and hot water stand up to the task) but doubles up well and makes for less stuff cluttering up the kitchen. An alternative is to use cupcake holders, or even a loaf tin from which you can cut oblong bars.

JUGS AND BOWLS

For anything involving beeswax it is best to have a separate jug or heatproof bowl dedicated to the cause. It requires high temperatures to melt and if you wash it down the sink it will likely solidify and block the pipes further down the line. I have a Pyrex jug and metal spoon that I use for all my beeswax recipes and then scrape the excess off at the end, once it is hard, and put it in a pot that I can later melt into a little dry skin balm with some oil and honey (see Beeswax and Honey Lip Balm, page 194). Working in this way does mean that sometimes a little crossover of ingredients and fragrances might occur between recipes but this is minimal, and can sometimes bring an added little *je ne sais quoi* to my body lotion bars or lip balm.

STORAGE

I avoid BPA-containing plastics and store all my leftover food in glass or ceramic storage containers. There are some great glass 'Tupperware' options coming on to the market, so it is worth researching the best value options before you buy, and old screw-top jars from previous purchases are also ideal. For homemade Nut Milk (see page 164), a glass bottle is ideal and can be re-used ad-infinitum. Kilner jars are also great to have in abundance – not only do they look lovely but they keep all our nuts, seeds, grains and coconut palm sugar safe, dry and easy to locate at all times. For natural beauty, a couple of jars are useful for natural deodorant and coconut oil; you will need a spray bottle for the Orange Flower Skin and Hair Spritz (see page 214), which you may already have, otherwise you can find some great recycled glass options online and the blue ones look especially lovely. The Everyday Body Wash (see page 197) can be stored in any screw-top bottle.

Part 1

FOOD

The key to committing to healthy cooking is a tried-and-tested repertoire of everyday recipes that are quick, uncomplicated and won't break the bank. A rainbow of fresh vegetables and fruit and a variety of nuts, seeds, nutritious grains and well-sourced eggs, meat and fish make up the majority of what follows, and if you can nail the everyday basics you will never be far from a healthy snack or meal. I try to avoid ready-made pastes, stocks and pastas as much as possible, and make what I can from scratch. Homemade stocks (see page 178), pestos (see pages 92, 109 and 121) and sauces like my favourite tahini one (see page 172) are my army of natural flavour enhancers. I hope these recipes encourage you to move away from shop-bought blends and notice the difference in flavour and how they make you feel.

In my own kitchen, time never seems to be on my side so my recipes are designed with busy people in mind. Many can be made in advance, and leftovers taken to work for lunch or re-hashed – simple additions like chopped herbs, toasted seeds or a couple of soft-boiled eggs and a dash of tamari can give yesterday's dinner a whole new lease of life. I will often prepare a few different salads or sides for one meal, or serve them with a dip and crackers or a sheet of seaweed: this maximises our nutrient intake, while incorporating exciting new ingredients, and whatever needs using up. My goal is never to get bored with healthy cooking; I hope you won't either.

The most important meal of the day! I believe in starting things as you mean to go on, and opening the morning with meditation and nutritious food paves the way for a harmonious and well-balanced waking day – both in terms of blood sugar and general mood. I love my sleep, and have never been one to leap out of bed and spend hours in the kitchen; instead I have come to rely on quick smoothies and breakfast bowls, packed with superfoods and fresh produce, to set me up for whatever the morning may bring. Otherwise, it's back to a giant coffee and nothing until lunch, and this does no one any favours. A nice routine is to make a herbal tea or hot water and lemon upon waking, meditate for 15 minutes or so and then eat a good breakfast. Staples like vanilla, almond butter, coconut and honey bring any smoothie blend to life and a good supply of frozen berries means that even when the fruit bowl is empty you won't fall short of breakfast material. In trying to reduce my sugar intake (and sweet tooth) I have become equally reliant on protein-rich, savoury, throw-it-all-in breakfast bowls (see my Salmon, Kale and Egg Bowl, page 54) and these are ideal fuel for busier days where more stamina is called for. I am also a big believer in piling on the toppings so feel free to throw on any powder, nut or supplement you want to be eating that day; I usually work around the recipes here and add some cacao or maca for an extra boost on demanding days. It is helpful, in whatever you are making for breakfast, to keep up the protein, fibre and fat content: these help us stay fuller for longer and avoid the blood sugar crashes often associated with sweet porridge or processed pastries. Nuts and seeds, coconut oil and chia seeds are all good morning allies, as are eggs with dark leafy greens. When buying breakfast on the move, keep it as wholefood and unprocessed as possible and check for any hidden sugars. A final tip is to take a smoothie in a bottle for a mid-morning energy top up.

90g gluten-free oats
500ml water
a small handful of kale, washed

a drizzle of olive or coconut oil
1 tbsp miso paste, or to taste
2 slices of ripe avocado

sesame seeds, to sprinkle

MISO PORRIDGE

VEGAN

Serves 4

With salty fermented miso and crispy kale, this exotic Asian-inspired porridge makes an exciting change from the traditional sweet version so many of us know and love. People always swoon at the unexpected flavours and moreish combination of creaminess and crunch. Miso may seem like an unusual breakfast choice but in Japan it is a staple in both traditional and modern cooking and used in a variety of dips, spreads, sauces, pickles and soups. Rich in fermented protein, it is also a good source of antioxidants and minerals, including zinc, copper, iron and manganese. Studies also show that despite its salty taste it does not raise blood pressure or stress the cardiovascular system in the same way that conventional salt does when ingested in equal quantities. I love its sweet, rich flavour and here you can add any greens you have to hand, or none at all. I like to balance the saltiness with a little creamy avocado – the extra calories will also keep you feeling fuller for longer.

In a pan, gently simmer the oats and water for about 10 minutes, stirring occasionally until the mixture is thick and creamy.

Meanwhile, shred a leaf or two of kale and gently brown in a pan with a small drizzle of oil. Less is more here, so if it's crispy but also a little uncooked that's perfect.

Stir the miso into the oats, adjusting to taste. Ladle into bowls and top with the crispy kale, sliced avocado and some sesame seeds sprinkled on top.

1 ripe banana, mashed
25g flaxseed, ground
2 tbsp almond butter
2 eggs
2 tbsp maple syrup

1 tbsp vanilla bean paste
1 tsp ground cinnamon
a pinch of salt
3 tbsp coconut oil

TO SERVE
Chia Berry Compote (see page 167)
maple syrup
sliced banana
nut butter

BANANA ALMOND PANCAKES

VEGETARIAN

Makes about
6 pancakes

I love pancakes because they remind me of America and in particular an amazing diner I went to on holiday in Lake Tahoe when I was a teenager – we would order stacks so huge I could never even finish them. I wanted to create a healthy alternative that was as close to the real thing as possible, not too heavy or packed with grains. This protein-rich version keeps you going until lunch and is versatile enough to go with both sweet and savoury accompaniments.

Combine all the ingredients except the coconut oil in a large bowl and mix thoroughly until smooth. Taste and add more maple syrup, cinnamon or salt if needed.

Melt a little of the coconut oil in a frying pan over a medium heat. Pour the mixture into small pancakes (about three at a time) and cook for 2–3 minutes; when lots of bubbles start to appear on the surface of the pancakes, flip them over and cook for a further minute or two until golden.

Transfer to a plate lined with kitchen paper while you cook the rest of the pancakes. Serve immediately with the Chia Berry Compote and extra maple syrup, banana and nut butter if desired.

2 apples, cored and quartered
  (or one apple and one carrot)
80g gluten-free oats
1–2 tbsp pumpkin seeds
200ml nut milk

1 tsp ground cinnamon
½ tsp vanilla bean paste
TOPPING SUGGESTIONS
(use as few or as many as you like)
nut butter

goji berries
bee pollen
coconut palm sugar
chia seeds

APPLE & CINNAMON BIRCHER MUESLI

RAW / VEGAN

Serves 2

Bircher muesli is an easy and affordable nutritional breakfast staple, and the traditional apple and cinnamon pairing is hard to beat. The beauty of bircher is that you can make it in batches that last for 2–3 days, and almost any fruit, nut or seed makes a welcome topping. The ones listed above are my go-to staples, and sometimes in winter I add a raw grated carrot with the apple and a little pinch of turmeric, or some stewed fruit and a sprinkling of nutmeg. Adding bee pollen will, of course, make this unsuitable if you are following a vegan diet.

In a bowl, grate the apples (or apple and carrot) and mix with the oats, pumpkin seeds, nut milk, cinnamon and vanilla. Cover and place in the fridge to soak overnight.

Serve with a dollop of nut butter and your favourite toppings.

80g cashews
200ml water
3 tbsp chia seeds
a pinch of ground cinnamon

1 tsp coconut oil, melted
1 tsp vanilla bean paste
1 tbsp coconut palm sugar
a small pinch of salt

goji berries
fresh fruit
desiccated coconut

CREAMY CASHEW CHIA

RAW / VEGAN

Serves 1
(or 2 with lots
of toppings)

This is about as creamy as plant food gets, and it makes for a surprisingly indulgent breakfast. The chia provides plenty of protein and fibre, while the coconut oil and cashew cream keep you sated all morning. Ground cinnamon balances blood sugar levels and helps keep mid-morning cravings at bay.

Again, you can add any topping to this; I usually go for the salty-sweet flavour of goji berries and some coconut, but fresh berries and fruit are just as delicious and even more nutritious.

Tip the cashews and water into a blender and process until smooth and creamy.

Pour into a bowl, add the remaining ingredients and set aside for 5–10 minutes to allow the chia seeds to absorb the liquid. Top with berries, fresh fruit or coconut and serve immediately.

FOOD HERO: CINNAMON

For me, cinnamon is the taste of winter and cosy, warming dishes that fight off frosty mornings and ever-longer evenings. Sprinkled on porridge, infused in warming tea blends, hung happily on Christmas trees in delicate scrolls of spicy bark: it always warms the heart and gives a unique flavour to everything it touches – both savoury and sweet. Its powerful, distinctive aroma brings a soft spiciness to any dish or drink and beneath its bold taste lies a wealth of healing benefits: it has been used since medieval times to treat all sorts of ailments, from infection and arthritis, to coughs and sore throats.

The spice is the brown, dry bark of the cinnamon tree, and it comes in raw stick form, ground into a powder or as an essential oil extract. It is a useful ingredient for curbing those all-too-familiar sugar cravings that so many of us fall prey to in between meals. It slows down our rate of digestion and reduces blood sugar spikes afterwards, and adding a good half teaspoonful to your porridge, muesli or other sweet treats will help you feel fuller and more sated for longer.

Cinnamon is also an anti-inflammatory spice: its compound cinnamaldehyde can help prevent platelets in the blood from clotting and can thus boost circulation and help protect against stroke, arterial and coronary disease. (On the reverse side, if you are on blood-thinning medication, you should seek medical advice before consuming large amounts of cinnamon.)

Cinnamon essential oil has antibacterial properties and the Egyptians used it as part of the mummification process for preservation. Research shows that when ingested, it can provide antiviral protection and slow the growth of fungi and yeast in the body that may be resistant to prescription drugs. The Egyptians and Romans are also reported to have used it to treat flatulence and indigestion, and it is still taken in tea or food for its carminative properties today: one teaspoonful of powdered bark per litre of water is recommended twice a day until symptoms subside.

Research has also shown that smelling or tasting cinnamon boosts cognitive function and increases alertness. All the more reason to sprinkle a little into your day.

Turn to page 71 to read about the benefits of turmeric and page 133 to read about ginger.

BREAKFAST

BREAKFAST

a large handful of spinach, washed
a small handful of kale, washed
a small handful of blueberries
   (fresh or frozen)

150–200ml nut milk
   or coconut water
1 tbsp nut butter
½ apple or pear, core removed

1 tsp spirulina powder
1 tsp vanilla bean paste

DAILY GREENS SMOOTHIE

RAW / VEGAN

Serves 4

The revered green smoothie single-handedly changed my life and to this day I feel stronger, lighter and brighter whenever I drink my greens. The cellulose plant fibre it provides is essential for proper detoxification and elimination, and the dense nutrient content of the dark leafy greens (especially high in iron and calcium) make it a powerful aid on the road to optimal wellness. Blending green leaves and a whole host of superfoods gives you all the benefits of the whole plant, while placing minimal strain on the digestive system. The result is a high-nutrient intake with less energy expenditure.

Coconut water gives a refreshing taste and good dose of electrolytes, while nut milk gives it a creamier flavour. Hardcore green devotees can leave out the fruit, but a little apple or pear goes a long way in the taste stakes.

Place all the ingredients in a blender and blitz until smooth. Drink immediately, or store in the fridge for up to 1 day.

4 eggs

FOR THE AVOCADO

1 ripe avocado, diced

a handful of fresh coriander leaves,
    plus extra to garnish

a handful of fresh parsley leaves,
    plus extra to garnish

juice of ½ lime

a drizzle of olive or hemp oil

salt and freshly ground black pepper

FOR THE BEANS

1 tbsp olive or coconut oil

1 large onion, finely chopped

1 large garlic clove, finely chopped

250g black beans, soaked in water
    overnight and boiled until tender

½ tsp smoked paprika, or to taste

1 tsp ground cumin

1 × 400g tin chopped tomatoes

1 tsp coconut palm sugar

¼ tsp ground cinnamon

¼ tsp cayenne pepper

salt and freshly ground black pepper

HEALTHY HUEVOS RANCHEROS

VEGETARIAN

Serves 4

This is a nutritional riff on my all-time favourite breakfast and the ultimate healthy hangover cure. Creamy avocado perfectly sets off the spicy beans, and plenty of parsley and coriander, both known to support the liver's detoxification process. Plus they give you a good dose of vitamin C. Add polenta or a corn tortilla for those incurable carb cravings.

To prepare the avocado, mix all of the ingredients together in a bowl, season to taste, cover and set aside while you prepare the beans.

Heat the oil in a large frying pan over a medium heat and sauté the onion and garlic until soft and golden. Add all the remaining ingredients and simmer for 5–10 minutes, or until the tomatoes have reduced to a nice thick consistency. Make four round spaces in the pan and crack an egg into each one. Continue to cook for 3–4 minutes, until the whites are firm.

Remove from the heat and divide between four plates. Top with the avocado mixture and season again with salt and pepper. Scatter with coriander and parsley leaves and serve immediately.

160g buckwheat groats
1 tsp ground cinnamon
450ml nut milk
a pinch of salt

2 tbsp desiccated coconut
1 tbsp honey
1 tsp vanilla bean paste

TOPPING SUGGESTIONS
nut butter, berries, fruit,
bee pollen, seeds, cacao nibs

BUCKWHEAT & COCONUT PORRIDGE

VEGETARIAN

Serves 2

On cold winter days you can't beat a bowl of sweet, creamy porridge and this grain-free buckwheat version is full of protein, vitamin B12 and blood-sugar-balancing cinnamon. With a lower glycaemic load than normal oats, it avoids the mid-morning hunger crash that we often fall prey to. Load yours with fruit, berries and superfoods (see page 26–30) in almost any combination. Cacao nibs and goji berries are my favourites.

Place the buckwheat, cinnamon and nut milk in a medium pan and bring to the boil. Reduce the heat and simmer for 15–20 minutes, until the buckwheat is soft and creamy but still retaining its shape and a little bite (you may need to add a little more milk or water to prevent it getting too thick).

Remove from the heat, stir in the remaining ingredients and serve warm with your chosen toppings.

250g berries, such as strawberries,
    raspberries, blueberries
150ml nut milk
½ ripe banana

2 tbsp cacao powder
1 tsp coconut oil
1 tsp acai powder

CACAO & BERRY SMOOTHIE

RAW / VEGAN

Serves 1

Berries go so well with the warm, bitter flavour of cacao but they are also little nutritional powerhouses, full of beneficial phytonutrients, the natural compounds found in plants that protect them from germs, fungi and other threats and that can perform a variety of beneficial functions in the body when ingested. Fruits and vegetables with a deep red, purple or blue hue also contain anthocyanins, pigments that are widely understood to have antioxidant properties. This is a great pick-me-up smoothie for any time of day and feels like a sumptuous chocolatey treat while still being wonderfully healthy – full of a whole host of essential vitamins and antioxidants. You can use frozen or fresh berries. Add a little maple syrup or honey to sweeten if desired, although, of course, honey isn't suitable for vegans.

Place all the ingredients in a blender and whizz until smooth and creamy. Taste and adjust with more honey, if needed.

1 garlic clove
2cm piece of fresh ginger, grated
2 tsp tamari, plus extra for drizzling
180g wild salmon fillet, skin on

2 eggs
a handful of pumpkin seeds
a handful of sunflower seeds
1 tbsp sesame seeds

olive or coconut oil, for frying
4 handfuls of kale, washed
4 tbsp hemp oil
freshly ground black pepper

SALMON, KALE & EGG BOWL

Serves 2

Transitioning from carb-based breakfasts to protein-based ones was one of the most dramatically beneficial moves I made when I started to eat more nutritionally. Bowls like this, with oily cold-water fish and plenty of fibrous greens, set you up with so much more fuel and energy for jam-packed days than refined carbohydrates or sugary cereals. The combination of tamari and hemp oil is one of my favourites and this dish would be just as good with the kale and them alone. The ginger and garlic add an extra Asian flavour.

Using a pestle and mortar, crush the garlic and ginger together and mix with the tamari. Pour into a bowl and add the salmon; cover and chill in the fridge for 15–20 minutes.

Bring a pan of water to the boil and soft-boil the eggs for 5½ minutes. Remove from the pan and run under cold water until cool enough to handle, then peel.

Meanwhile, lightly toast the seeds in a dry frying pan until golden, then set aside.

When you're ready to serve, fry the salmon skin side down in a little olive or coconut oil over a medium heat for 4–5 minutes, then turn and cook for another 3–4 minutes, until it is cooked through and flakes easily. Remove from the heat and allow to cool before removing the skin and breaking into chunks.

Chop and steam the kale over a pan of boiling water for just 1 minute, then drizzle with hemp oil and tamari. Divide between two bowls and add the flaked salmon. Break an egg on top, sprinkle with the toasted seeds and finish with some black pepper.

1 heaped tbsp acai powder
2 bananas
a handful of berries
1 tsp nut butter

250ml nut milk or coconut water
1 tsp coconut oil
2 tbsp desiccated coconut

a handful of chopped fresh fruit
a sprinkling of chia, pumpkin or
    sunflower seeds or almonds
4–5 fresh mint leaves

ACAI SMOOTHIE BOWL

RAW / VEGAN

Serves 2

Smoothie bowls offer a really substantial blended breakfast and are fun to decorate with energy-giving fruits, seeds and healthy sprinkles. When throwing them together, I rely entirely on what I have in the kitchen and have never made two the same. Here are some of my favourite topping combinations but you can play around with what you like and mix it up.

The acai berry from Brazil gives us both potent antioxidant protection from free-radical damage and a beautiful purple colour – it's a smoothie bowl's best friend.

Place all the ingredients in a blender and whizz until smooth and creamy. Taste and adjust if necessary, adding more of whatever you think it needs.

Pour into bowls, scatter over your chosen toppings and serve immediately.

No.02

HEALTHY
TREATS

Snacking is important, nutritionally speaking, and too fun not to do. The world of snacks is never ending and devising healthy versions of childhood favourites was one of my favourite parts of writing The Naturalista.

There are so many delicious ways to curb those mid-morning and afternoon hunger dips and working hugely inconsistent hours for so long in street food turned me into something of a snack junkie. It also burned a huge hole in my pocket. Homemade energy balls, superfood drinks, granola bars and muffins are affordable alternatives to shop-bought options and all come to the rescue when weakness suddenly hits and you think you want a Snickers. The only thing they require is a small amount of planning – although my Mayan Superfood Hot Chocolate (see page 78) or Spiced Turmeric and Nutmeg Milk (page 68) are as speedy to make as a cafetière of coffee and keep kids and adults away from the processed snack-crack that has such disastrous effects on our health. Things to nibble on the go are also important for keeping energy levels stable, and with a few little twists they can be much more exciting than plain nuts and berries: a sprinkling of coconut palm sugar, a quick roast and dash of black pepper, smoked paprika and tamari, a dusting of cacao and cinnamon are all quick and easy ways to produce heaps of tasty snack material with minimal effort or forethought.

FOR THE BASE
100g ground almonds
3 tbsp coconut oil
1 tbsp nut butter
1 tbsp honey
1 tsp vanilla bean paste
a pinch of sea salt

APRICOT AND COCONUT
20g desiccated coconut,
    plus extra to dust
60g dried unsulphured apricots,
    roughly chopped

CACAO SUPERFOOD
1 tbsp bee pollen
4 tbsp cacao powder,
    plus extra to dust
1 tsp spirulina powder

1 tsp wheatgrass powder
4 cardamom pods, shelled
    and seeds crushed
¼ tsp ground cinnamon

MACA, GOJI AND GINGER
1 tbsp maca powder
2 tsp ground ginger, or to taste
1 tbsp desiccated coconut
30g dried goji berries, pulsed
    in a blender

POWER
BALLS

RAW / VEGETARIAN

Makes about
12 balls

Delicious though they are, shop-bought power balls cost an accumulative fortune and are often full of hidden refined sugars, protein powders and other binders. As a devoted snacker all day, every day, I came up with a basic power ball recipe that can be adapted in infinite combinations. Here are my favourite three. Whether I'm craving a cacao hit or just using up what's in the kitchen, this one-size-fits-all recipe ensures I'm never far from a healthy and affordable sweet treat. If you prefer more bite and sweetness, add some pulsed dates and use a little less of the ground almond.

Place the base ingredients in a large mixing bowl and add your chosen combination of ingredients. Mix well and then roll into bite-sized balls. Chill in the fridge for 20–30 minutes before eating.

HEALTHY TREATS

120g quinoa
1 small apple, cored,
    peeled and quartered
2 ripe medium bananas, mashed
1 egg

2 tbsp coconut palm sugar
2 tbsp coconut oil
25g gluten-free oats
1 tsp ground cinnamon
1 tsp baking powder

1 tsp vanilla bean paste
a pinch of salt
1 tbsp chia seeds
125g blueberries

QUINOA BLUEBERRY MUFFINS

VEGETARIAN

Makes about
10 muffins

A good muffin is an integral part of any teatime repertoire and these quinoa blueberry ones are yummy little parcels of joy whatever the time of day.

The secret to the moist texture is a little apple purée – quick and easy to make while your quinoa boils and packs in some extra nutrients.

Preheat the oven to 180°C/gas 4 and lightly grease a 12-hole muffin tray (or line with muffin cases).

Start by rinsing your quinoa thoroughly in cold water. Add to a pan with double the volume of water and bring to the boil. Cover, reduce the heat and simmer for about 15 minutes or so, until the white rings start falling away from the grain but it is still firm with a little bite. Remove from the heat, rinse again, drain and set aside in a large bowl to cool.

Meanwhile, place the apple pieces in a small pan with just enough water to cover and simmer over a low-medium heat for about 5 minutes, or until softened. Remove from the heat, drain and mash to create 2 tablespoons of purée.

Tip the quinoa and apple purée into a large mixing bowl, add all the remaining ingredients except the chia seeds and blueberries and mix thoroughly. Add the chia seeds, mix again, then stir in the blueberries.

Spoon into the muffin cases or muffin tray and bake in the oven for 40 minutes, or until golden on top. Transfer to a wire rack to cool.

Store in an airtight container for up to 3 days.

6 dates (look for the Deglet
  Nour variety)
1 tbsp flaxseed
2 tbsp sesame seeds

15 blanched almonds or cashews,
  ideally soaked in water for at
  least 8 hours
½ tsp chia seeds

500ml water
1 tsp turmeric
½ tsp grated nutmeg

SPICED TURMERIC & NUTMEG MILK

RAW / VEGAN

Serves 2

Turmeric is a powerful natural antioxidant with anti-inflammatory properties, thanks to its brilliant bright yellow flavonoid, curcumin (for more information, see Food Heroes on page 71). This spicy drink brings it to life with sweet dates and fragrant, antibacterial nutmeg, while omega-filled sesame and flax provide good nourishing oils and plenty of long-lasting energy.

If you have a high-speed blender, you can use almonds or cashews here; if not, cashews are easier to break down and a better option for a smooth texture.

Place all the ingredients in a blender and whizz until smooth and creamy. Serve immediately.

FOOD HERO: TURMERIC

Turmeric's wonderful bright yellow pigment, curcumin, has powerful anti-inflammatory and antioxidant effects in the body, and while it has been a mainstay of ancient medicine and Ayurveda for centuries, modern western food culture has only recently started to pay proper homage to its healing powers.

The plant grows as a root and you can buy it whole, or dried and powdered. Its distinctive flavour and colour add depth to both savoury and sweet dishes, and I use it in a wide range of recipes, from dahl and tagines to a sweet, spicy milk (see pages 103, 106 and 68). When ingested, curcumin has been shown to inhibit the action of a number of enzymes involved in the body's inflammatory response, most importantly COX-2 and 5-LOX, which play an important role in inflammation, and is used as both a culinary addition and a naturopathic supplement to treat conditions such as arthritis, swelling and joint pain. Research also shows that curcumin can increase cellular levels of glutathione: an important antioxidant that helps our cells adapt to stress. Turmeric also contains compounds that can help protect the structure of our cell membranes, protecting against the mutations and changes that can cause disease and cancer, and is praised for its ability to cleanse the blood of toxins.

As with all foods that provide healing properties within the bodies, turmeric is a great anti-inflammatory aid because it does not produce side effects; often we take painkillers and NSAIDs (non-steroidal anti-inflammatory drugs, like ibuprofen) without considering the pay-off that occurs within us when we do – the risk of gastric upset and damage to the liver and kidneys.

Curcumin is not as 'bioavailable', however, as some other medicinal foods – meaning that its actual absorption and uptake by the gut can be minimal compared with the amount ingested (it is metabolised very fast by the liver and the intestine.) Studies have shown, however, that when eaten with black pepper, its absorption is dramatically increased.

It is also used in many cultures as a topical analgesic, to provide relief to rheumatoid and skin inflammation when applied as a paste. Simply mix a little powder or blended root with water or oil (sesame, almond or olive work well), spread on the inflamed areas and leave for 15–20 minutes before rinsing off. Some people also swear by using it as a face mask, but be aware that the yellow pigment can often leave its mark…

Always buy organic turmeric, and seek medical advice before taking it in supplement form.

Turn to page 44 to read about the benefits of cinnamon and page 133 to read about ginger.

5 large dates (look for the
    Deglet Nour variety)
30g chia seeds
35g nut butter

1 tsp coconut oil
20g desiccated coconut
2 tbsp cacao powder
1 tbsp honey

a pinch of salt
optional extras: 1 tsp cacao nibs,
    maca powder, spirulina powder,
    bee pollen

RAW CHIA CHOCOLATE FUDGE

RAW / VEGETARIAN

Makes 8–10
bite-sized
chunks

I have tried a vast array of healthy fudges in my time and this chocolate one takes the biscuit. The chia gives it a good portion of fibre while the chewy, sweet dates are as close to the real deal as you can get.

If you have a high-speed blender you have the option of pulverising the chia seeds to make a finer fudge. If you are using a food processor you will have crunchier pieces: both are delicious and I make it both ways. The recipe is wonderfully versatile too, so you can add a teaspoon or two of whatever superfoods you like (maca for an energy boost, bee pollen or spirulina for some extra protein and nutrients) and they will blend in easily: perfect for picky kids – or grown-ups.

Place the dates and chia seeds in a blender or food processor and pulse until well combined. Add the remaining ingredients, including any optional extras, and pulse again to combine thoroughly until a dough-like mixture forms.

Line a small Tupperware or dish, approx 12 × 18cm, with baking parchment or cling film (or spread evenly into a non-stick tray). Spoon the mixture into the dish, press into the edges and place in the fridge to set. When firm, cut into chunks and keep in the fridge for up to 5 days.

2 tbsp coconut oil
4 large dates, roughly chopped
   (look for the Deglet Nour variety)
8 dried figs, roughly chopped
3 ripe bananas

1 tsp vanilla bean paste
2 tbsp maple syrup
1 tsp ground cinnamon
a pinch of salt
140g gluten-free oats

60g pumpkin seeds
60g sunflower seeds
40g buckwheat (optional)
70g almonds, roughly chopped

BANANA, FIG & DATE GRANOLA BARS

VEGAN

Makes about
10 bars

This recipe uses bananas to bind a whole host of other delicious plant-based ingredients. When I make a batch I end up taking them everywhere with me – they are the perfect snack for any time of day and an especially good breakfast-on-the-run. Dried figs are a rich source of calcium, which is great for vegans and especially children who love their sweet flavour and chewy bite. I add buckwheat when I have it for some extra protein and crunch but it works just as well without.

Preheat the oven to 180°C/gas 4 and line a baking tray approximately 23 × 32cm with baking parchment (or use a non-stick tray).

Melt the coconut oil in a small pan over a low heat, add the dates and figs and heat gently for 5 minutes until soft. Remove from the heat and leave to cool while you prepare the rest of the ingredients.

Place the bananas in a blender and whizz until they are creamy. Transfer to a large mixing bowl and stir in the vanilla bean paste, maple syrup, cinnamon and salt. Then add the remaining ingredients, including the figs and dates, and mix thoroughly.

Spread out in your prepared tray and bake in the oven for 25–30 minutes, or until the edges are nice and golden. Remove from the oven, cool and then remove from the tin and slice into rectangular bars. Store in an airtight container or wrapped in baking parchment for up to 3 days.

60g sunflower seeds
60g pumpkin seeds
45g gluten-free oats
6 large dates (look for the
    Deglet Nour variety)

1 tbsp grated fresh ginger
30g cacao nibs
2 tbsp coconut oil
1 tbsp hemp flour
60–80g honey or maple syrup

20g desiccated coconut
1 tsp wheatgrass powder
1 tsp spirulina powder
1 tbsp maca powder
10g flaxseed

RAW GREEN ENERGY BARS

RAW / VEGETARIAN

Makes
8–10 bars

When creating these bars, I wanted to harness the abundance of nutrients in my two favourite green powders – spirulina and wheatgrass – without compromising on flavour. I also wanted to create an energy bar that was not dependent on nuts, as so many on the shelves often are. Marrying spicy fresh ginger, omega-rich seeds and energy-boosting cacao, maca and hemp protein, this is the result.

Honey works best to bind the mixture but if you are vegan you can use maple syrup instead. I recommend starting with less rather than more, and adding to taste. The beauty of raw food is that you can adjust as you go and these bars can be customised to suit all types of sweet tooth.

Place the sunflower and pumpkin seeds, oats, dates, ginger and 20g of the cacao nibs in a food processor and pulse until a chunky mixture comes together.

Pour into a mixing bowl and stir in the remaining ingredients. The dough should be thick and sticky – if you need more moisture, add a little more grated ginger and if it is too liquid, add some more oats or flaxseed.

Line a small tupperware or tray, about 26 × 18cm, with baking parchment and spoon the mixture in, pressing it down with your hands to make a flat layer about 2cm thick. Place in the fridge to set for 20 minutes then slice into bars.

Store the bars in the fridge in an airtight container for up to 1 week.

HEALTHY TREATS

HEALTHY TREATS

500ml nut milk
3 tbsp raw cacao powder
3 dates, pitted (look for
   the Deglet Nour variety)

1 tbsp hemp seeds or 5 macadamias
1 tsp ground cinnamon
½ tsp cayenne pepper
2 drops orange essential oil

honey or coconut palm sugar,
   to sweeten
a pinch of salt

MAYAN SUPERFOOD HOT CHOCOLATE

VEGETARIAN

Serves 2

Cacao, orange, spice and an imperceptible touch of salt: all the kicks you need to ramp up a sluggish afternoon, and so good for you too. This healthy hot chocolate is heaven in a cup.

If you are really in need of some TLC, you can also add a little dried reishi powder: this healing medicinal mushroom blends in well with the warming cinnamon and is brilliant for calming the nervous system and promoting relaxation – just what hot choc moments call for.

Place all the ingredients in a blender and whizz until smooth. Transfer to a pan and warm gently over a low heat before serving.

HEALTHY TREATS

40g sunflower seeds
50g pumpkin seeds
50g flaxseed

25g chia seeds
1 tbsp olive oil
1 tbsp nutritional yeast

1 tbsp bee pollen
125ml water
a pinch of salt

OMEGA SEED CRACKERS

VEGETARIAN

Makes about 10 cracker bites

A great cracker base is a must for anyone transitioning from a bread-fuelled lifestyle to a wholefood one. This versatile recipe contains an abundance of omegas and is wonderfully easy, without the need for a dehydrator. You can add a teaspoon of honey and cinnamon for a sweeter riff, while a good pinch of dried herbs, sprinkle of turmeric or ground cumin and a splash of tamari or 2–3 diced sundried tomatoes give you something spicy and salty. Play around with variations – I tend to go with whatever is on the cupboard shelf and make batches to store so we are never short of a healthy snack to nibble. (I like to use them to scoop up Baba Ganoush or my Smoky Beet Hummus, see page 125.) You can also leave out the bee pollen for a vegan cracker. I bake these on a re-usable non-stick baking sheet but any non-stick baking paper will work.

Preheat the oven to 150°C/gas 2.

Mix all the ingredients in a bowl and leave to soak for 20–30 minutes until a dough-like mixture forms. (If it is too runny you can add a little extra chia and leave for another 10 minutes.)

Roll out as thinly as possible on a non-stick silicone or baking paper sheet. This is easiest if you place the mixture between two sheets and roll it flat with a rolling pin then gently peel off the top sheet.

Bake in the oven for 45 minutes, or until golden and crisp, checking regularly for the last 10 minutes. They should be crisp all the way through but make sure they do not start to burn.

Remove from the oven and allow to cool before breaking into crackers. Store in an airtight container for up to 4 days.

My inherently eclectic approach to cooking means that I often like to make a variety of dishes as a main course, and many of these recipes are designed to be served with one another or one or two salads or sides. Others are more substantial and bring an often-needed cut of meat or fish to the table – see the Miso and Green Chilli Chicken Skewers (page 95) or Lamb Tagine with Cauliflower and Parsnip Couscous (page 106). This is born of a continual desire to try out new things while using up leftovers and fruit and vegetables that need eating up, and often unexpected ideas and flavours come together in a way I would never have imagined. I like to cook like this because it keeps me learning, minimises waste and encourages me to eat a wider variety of ingredients. It also allows for a more nutritionally complete way of eating than the traditional meat and two veg scenario: protein-packed Wild Salmon and Quinoa Cakes (see page 100) or Cornershop Dahl (page 103) alongside Miso Almond Greens (page 130) or Kale and Avocado Rice with Pickled Carrot (page 117) – add some probiotic sauerkraut (page 177) and Omega Seed Crackers (page 81) on the side and you have a rich, varied and well-balanced plate. These recipes also draw on different cuisines from around the world, although from our journey with Rainbo, Asian-inspired flavour combinations often take front seat – particularly with meat and fish where they really come to life.

1 tbsp coconut oil
2 sweetcorn cobs, kernels
   removed and rinsed
1 onion, diced

1 red pepper, deseeded and diced
1 × 400ml tin coconut milk
400ml vegetable stock
a pinch of saffron strands

¼ tsp smoked paprika
salt and freshly ground black pepper
snipped chives, to garnish

CORN & COCONUT CHOWDER

VEGAN

Serves 2 as a
main or 4 as
a starter

I was brought up on my mother's corn and smoked haddock chowder and the cosy memory of it on Friday nights at home around the Aga will stay with me forever. Here I have adapted that nourishing comforting soup to be plant-based, but her secret ingredient still remains: a little pinch of saffron. It goes so well with the sweet, crunchy corn and creamy coconut. This rich bowl of goodness has become a quick and easy staple in our house and shows no signs of fading.

Melt the coconut oil in a pan over a medium hat and gently sauté the corn kernels, onion and pepper in the coconut oil until soft and golden. Remove from the heat and tip into a blender. Add the coconut milk, vegetable stock and spices and gently pulse until the soup is creamy but still has a chunky texture.

Season to taste with salt and pepper, then warm through in a pan for a few minutes before serving with a sprinkling of snipped chives.

680g rump or sirloin steak, trimmed and cut into 3cm-wide strips
3 tbsp coconut oil, for frying
Asian Rainbow Slaw (see page 131)
FOR THE MARINADE
2 garlic cloves, chopped
thumb-sized piece of fresh ginger, grated

¼ tsp smoked paprika
½ tsp ground cumin
½ tsp ground cinnamon
1 tbsp lime juice
1 tbsp coconut oil
a pinch of salt
FOR THE SATAY SAUCE
100g roasted cashews
1 small shallot, finely chopped

juice of ½ lime
1 stalk lemongrass, minced
1 tbsp coconut palm sugar
1 tbsp tamari
150ml coconut milk
thumb-sized piece of fresh ginger, grated
1 small red chilli, deseeded and roughly chopped

CASHEW BEEF SATAY WITH RAINBOW SLAW

Serves 2 as a main or 4 as a starter

The smell of smoky griddled beef instantly transports me to a bustling food market and this healthy take on a classic satay takes us right back to sunny street food Friday nights with Rainbo, where skewers, slaw and endless supplies of cold beer were all anyone needed.

Sweet cashew satay is one of my favourite ways to eat beef and perfectly complements the spicy marinade. Cooked at a high heat and perfectly tender on the inside, it doesn't get any better. The beef can be marinated a good few hours in advance but the satay sauce is best prepared just before serving.

Mix the marinade ingredients together in a non-metallic bowl and add the beef. Rub thoroughly to make sure it is well combined, then thread the beef strips onto skewers, cover and place in the fridge for 3–4 hours.

To make the satay sauce, pulse all the ingredients together in a blender or food processor until creamy but still a little chunky; you want the cashews to still have some bite. You may want to add more coconut milk or water if it is too thick. Transfer to a pan and cook gently over a low heat for 5 minutes. Set aside to cool.

Place a griddle pan over a high heat and brush with a little coconut oil. Cook the beef, seasoning each skewer with salt as you go. It is best to take one or two cubes and try them out to see how long they need: I usually griddle one side for about 3 minutes and then turn and cook for another 2 minutes on the other side. You want the meat to be nicely grilled on the outside but pink and tender in the middle.

Serve with the satay sauce and some Asian Rainbow Slaw on the side, or remove the beef from the skewers and serve in cabbage or kale leaves or with some greens.

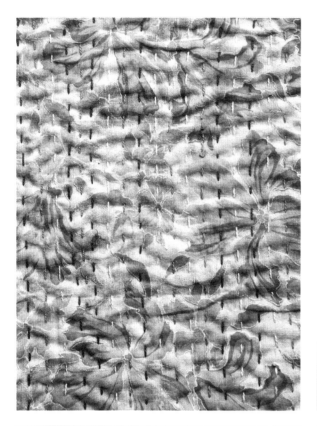

MAINS

3 large courgettes, halved and sliced
  lengthways with a mandoline or
  vegetable peeler
1 bowl of Cashew Cream Cheese
  (see page 168)
200g cherry tomatoes, halved
  and lightly salted
a large handful of rocket

FOR THE GREEN PESTO
2 handfuls of kale, washed
2 handfuls of spinach, washed
15 almonds, ideally soaked
  in water for at least 8 hours
2 tbsp pumpkin seeds
2 tbsp olive oil
2 heaped tsp nutritional yeast
1 small garlic clove
1 tbsp lemon juice
salt and freshly ground black pepper

FOR THE RED PESTO
½ small shallot
15 sundried tomatoes
1 tsp apple cider vinegar
3 tbsp olive oil
5 cherry tomatoes
2 tbsp sunflower seeds
5 sprigs of fresh oregano
1 date, pitted (look for the
  Deglet Nour variety)
salt and freshly ground black pepper

RAW COURGETTE LASAGNE

RAW / VEGAN

Serves 4

Although this raw lasagne has a few components, they are all very quick to prepare and it is such a fun meal to put together with friends. Piling up the courgette and pesto layers can become quite an artistic endeavour, and some healthy competition is encouraged: no two plates ever come out the same. I was taught this recipe by raw chef Diego Castro and the balance of sweet, salty and acidic elements running through the two pestos creates a lovely depth of flavour, while the creamy cashew brings an extra nutty sweetness to complement the crunchy courgette strips. If you're short on time, you can prepare all the sauces in advance so you just need to slice the vegetables before serving.

Place the ingredients for the green pesto in a food processor or blender and whizz until smooth but still a little chunky. Taste and adjust the seasoning then transfer to a bowl, cover and place in the fridge until needed. Repeat to make the red pesto.

Serve all the components on the table and invite your guests to create their own towers, alternating three layers of courgette slices, green and red pesto and cashew cream cheese. Garnish with cherry tomatoes, rocket and ground black pepper.

1 red pepper, deseeded
6 large tomatoes
1 small fennel bulb, cored

1 cucumber
2 small garlic cloves,
    roughly chopped

1 tbsp olive oil
1 tbsp apple cider vinegar
salt and freshly ground black pepper

5-MINUTE FENNEL GAZPACHO

RAW / VEGAN

Serves 2 as a
main or 4 as
a starter

*I studied modern languages at university and spent five months
living in Seville. Under the blazing Andalusian sun I consumed
so much gazpacho, with so much fervour – I couldn't fathom
why we don't all drink our salads everywhere. The arrival
of the green smoothie is some progress, but when you need a
savoury hit of tomato and garlic, nothing quite beats the ice-cold
summer soup.*

*I have added fennel here for some gentle sweetness; you
could also throw in some ripe watermelon. Garnishes can range
from leftover croutons to hard-boiled eggs, capers, herbs, spring
onion, jamón – in fact pretty much anything you feel like.
In the summer I take this in a thermos with me around the city;
it beats hot coffee every time.*

Roughly chop the pepper, tomatoes, fennel and cucumber into chunks.
Add to a food processor or blender with all the remaining ingredients and
blitz on high speed until smooth.

Taste and adjust the seasoning. Transfer to a bowl, cover and chill in the
fridge until needed.

Serve very cold with any garnishes you like (see recipe introduction).

450g boneless, skinless chicken thighs, cut into 3cm pieces

FOR THE MARINADE

2 tbsp sesame oil

4 tbsp mirin

70g miso paste

1–2 large green chillies, finely chopped

FOR THE CORIANDER MATCHA SAUCE

4 tbsp olive oil

1 tbsp rice vinegar, or to taste

½ tsp matcha powder

a pinch of chilli flakes

60g fresh coriander

a dash of tamari

1 small garlic clove

MISO & GREEN CHILLI CHICKEN SKEWERS

Serves 3–4 with a side

Another Rainbo favourite, this spicy miso marinade is the perfect accompaniment to some tender chicken thighs. The salty sweetness of the miso and the heat of the green chilli really bring the meat to life; these flavourings can also be used with minced chicken thigh for homemade gyoza.

The coriander matcha sauce is full of antioxidants and fresh Asian flavours, with a spicy touch of red chilli to complement the chicken.

Whisk or blend all the marinade ingredients together in a large bowl until smooth. Add the chicken pieces and mix to ensure each one is well coated. Place in the fridge to marinate for at least 20 minutes and then skewer up.

Preheat the oven to 180°C/gas 4.

Place all the ingredients for the sauce in a food processor or blender and blitz to make a sauce. Taste and adjust the seasoning.

Arrange the chicken skewers on a non-stick baking tray and cook in the oven for 20–25 minutes, or until golden and cooked through, turning them halfway through the cooking time.

Serve immediately with the coriander matcha sauce.

1 beetroot, peeled
1 small butternut squash, peeled
    and chopped into wedges
3 tbsp olive or coconut oil
½ leek

150g buckwheat noodles
sea salt

FOR THE PASTE
3 tbsp pumpkin and/or
    sunflower seeds

70g roasted sesame seeds
1 tbsp maple syrup, or to taste
1 tbsp toasted sesame oil
1 tbsp tamari, or to taste
2 tbsp brown rice vinegar

BUCKWHEAT NOODLE BOWL WITH ROASTED BUTTERNUT & BEETROOT

VEGAN

Serves 2

This hearty bowl of sweet sesame deliciousness never fails to turn a stressful day around. The nutty buckwheat noodles can be bought at most supermarkets or health food stores, and they are a delicious protein-rich alternative to their refined rice or wheat counterparts.

The paste looks especially striking if you use black sesame seeds, but white is equally tasty.

Preheat the oven to 180°C/gas 4.

Place the beetroot and butternut squash in a roasting tray with 2 tablespoons of the olive or coconut oil and a sprinkling of salt. Roast for about 20 minutes, or until golden. Remove from the oven, chop the beetroot into rough chunks and set aside to cool.

Meanwhile, slice your leek lengthways and finely shred it into thin strips. Heat the remaining oil in a small frying pan over a medium heat and sauté the leeks until brown and crispy. Remove from the pan, drain on kitchen paper and set aside to cool.

Next make the paste by pounding all the ingredients together in a pestle and mortar (or use a small food processor). Taste and add more tamari or maple syrup, if desired.

Cook your buckwheat noodles in boiling water according to the packet instructions. Drain and stir in three-quarters of the paste. Serve in bowls with the roasted vegetables and the rest of the paste piled on top, garnished with the shredded fried leeks.

2 large onions
1 large or 2 small butternut squash,
 peeled and roughly chopped
½ tsp ground cumin

2 tbsp coconut oil
12 chestnut mushrooms, sliced
1 tsp turmeric
a handful of rocket or alfalfa sprouts

1 ripe avocado, sliced
salt and freshly ground black pepper

BUTTERNUT EXPRESS SOUP

VEGAN

Serves 2

I learned to make these bowls from one of the most amazing nutritional chefs I know, Diego Castro. He knocked them up at a yoga retreat on a chilly spring evening and they were pure heaven – and so quick to assemble. It is a last-minute favourite at home when a hug in a bowl is needed, and fast. You can improvise with the toppings but the turmeric mushrooms and peppery rocket are the perfect starting point, with a scoop of ripe avocado on top. Tamari seeds, alfalfa sprouts, shredded leeks and lots of parsley are also great additions.

Be sure to add plenty of black pepper when cooking the mushrooms: it increases the absorption of turmeric and its anti-inflammatory benefits.

Roughly chop one of the onions and place it in a large pan with the butternut squash. Add the ground cumin and just enough water to cover and bring to the boil over a medium-high heat. Cook for 10–15 minutes, or until the squash is soft. Remove from the heat and transfer to a food processor or blender. Blitz until you have a smooth soup and season to taste, adding a little more water or some vegetable stock if it is too thick.

Meanwhile, slice the remaining onion. Melt the coconut oil in a frying pan over a medium-high heat and fry the sliced onion and mushrooms with the turmeric and a generous amount of freshly ground black pepper for 7–8 minutes or until golden.

Ladle the warm soup into bowls and top with the turmeric mushrooms, rocket and sliced avocado. Finish with more freshly ground black pepper.

55g quinoa
240g skinless wild salmon fillet
2 tbsp gluten-free oats
20g toasted sesame seeds

1 egg, beaten
2 spring onions, finely chopped
large thumb-sized piece of
    fresh ginger, grated

2 garlic cloves, crushed
1 tbsp tamari
1 tbsp sesame oil
3 tbsp coconut or olive oil, for frying

WILD SALMON & QUINOA CAKES

Serves 2 as a
main or 4 as
a starter

These tasty little Asian wild salmon cakes are loaded with extra protein from the quinoa. The rich flavours of the sesame and ginger really bring the fish to life and I love the contrast between the rich meaty texture and the crunchy sautéed quinoa crust. As with most grains, the key is to try not to overcook the quinoa so that it retains some bite and texture.

They are delicious hot or cold, so make up a batch and keep for lunches on the go, or serve for busy weekday dinners.

Start by rinsing your quinoa thoroughly in cold water. Add to a pan with double the volume of water and bring to the boil. Cover, reduce the heat and simmer for about 15 minutes or so, until the white rings start falling away from the grain but it is still firm with a little bite. Remove from the heat, rinse again, drain and set aside in a large bowl to cool.

Meanwhile, cut the salmon into small chunks (the smaller the better so that the cakes hold together). When the quinoa is cool, add all the ingredients except the coconut oil to it and mix together until well combined, adding more oats if the cakes are a little moist. Form into 8–10 palm-sized patties and place in the fridge for 15–20 minutes to chill.

When you are ready, heat the coconut or olive oil in a frying pan over a medium-high heat and fry the patties for 6–8 minutes on each side, until crisp and golden brown. Drain on kitchen paper and serve warm or cold with a salad or some veggies (see Tamari Chard, Green Bitters Salad with Nigella and Nasturtiums, Asian Rainbow Slaw, pages 120, 126 and 131).

MAINS

250g short-grain brown rice
500ml vegetable stock
500g dried red lentils
1 tbsp olive or coconut oil
1 onion, thinly sliced
2 garlic cloves, crushed

2 tsp ground cumin
1 tsp ground coriander
1½ tsp turmeric
1 × 400g tin coconut milk
1 × 400g tin chopped tomatoes
150g kale, washed and chopped

a handful of chopped fresh parsley,
    to garnish
sea salt and freshly ground black
    pepper

CORNERSHOP DAHL

VEGAN

Serves 4

This quick and delicious recipe was born of an urgent craving on a cold winter's night, and the only ingredients our local shop had to offer. A pantry staple, turmeric is key for winter health as it is a potent anti-inflammatory, while one serving of humble red lentils provides us with around 90% of our daily folate needs (vital for almost all of our bodily systems). Brown rice and greens make hearty healthy sides. May it transform cold Monday nights forever more.

Start by cooking the rice in a pan of boiling water over a medium heat until soft but still with some bite (it should take about the same time it takes to make the dahl).

Bring the vegetable stock to the boil in a pan and add the lentils. Simmer for 20 minutes, stirring regularly.

Meanwhile melt the olive or coconut oil in a frying pan over a medium heat and lightly fry the onion and garlic for 1 minute until they begin to soften. Add the spices and continue to fry for another minute until they are nice and golden.

Add to the pan of lentils, along with the coconut milk and chopped tomatoes. Continue to cook, stirring regularly, until the lentils are all soft but not quite broken down (you may want to add a little water if you like a thinner consistency). Season to taste with salt and pepper.

Lightly steam the kale for a few minutes. Drain the rice and serve in bowls with the dahl and steamed kale, garnished with fresh parsley.

300g uncooked beetroot, peeled and roughly chopped
1 tbsp olive or avocado oil
40g hazelnuts (skin on)
350g new potatoes, halved
1 fennel bulb, finely sliced

4 smoked mackerel fillets, skinned and broken into small chunks
a small handful of dill
sea salt

FOR THE DRESSING
1 tbsp cold-pressed olive oil

2 tbsp capers
juice of 1 lemon
grated zest of ½ lemon
1 small red chilli, deseeded and finely chopped
salt and freshly ground black pepper

SMOKED MACKEREL, BEETROOT & FENNEL SALAD

Serves 2 as a main or 4 as a starter

In naturopathic nutrition we encourage eating oily, coldwater fish as they are full of anti-inflammatory Omega-3 fatty acids. We also like to keep our veggies varied and 'eat the rainbow'. This delicious salad covers both, and makes a light yet nourishing main course packed with protein and crunch. I like to buy pepper-coated mackerel for extra spice and warmth. If you're really hungry, you can also add a quartered soft-boiled egg for extra protein.

Preheat the oven to 180°C/gas 4 while you prepare the vegetables.

Toss the beetroot in the olive or avocado oil on a roasting tray, season with a little salt and roast for 15–20 minutes, until soft but still firm to the bite. At the same time, roast the hazelnuts on a separate tray for 10 minutes, or until they are lightly toasted and their skins start to crack. When done, remove from the oven and set both of the trays aside to cool.

Meanwhile, cook the potatoes in boiling salted water over a medium heat for 10 minutes, or until tender. Drain and set aside to cool.

To prepare the dressing, whisk together the olive oil, capers, lemon juice and zest and chilli and season with salt and pepper.

Tip the cooled potatoes and sliced fennel into a bowl, pour over the dressing and mix well. Divide between plates and top with the roasted beetroot and mackerel chunks. Garnish with dill and toasted hazelnuts.

2 tbsp olive oil
2 red onions, roughly chopped
750g lamb neck, cut into 2.5cm cubes
1 tsp ground cumin
heaped ½ tsp ground cinnamon
heaped ½ tsp ground ginger
a pinch of turmeric
a pinch of cayenne pepper

1 × 400g tin chopped tomatoes
150ml stock, or more if needed
70g dried unsulphured apricots, roughly chopped
1 tsp salt (or more to taste)

FOR THE COUSCOUS
½ large or 1 small cauliflower, broken into florets

3 parsnips, peeled
1 small red chilli, finely chopped
2 tsp ground cumin, or to taste
2 tbsp olive oil
a handful of fresh parsley, roughly chopped, plus extra to serve
2 tbsp pomegranate seeds (optional)
salt and freshly ground black pepper

LAMB TAGINE WITH CAULIFLOWER & PARSNIP COUSCOUS

Serves 3–4

Lamb, cinnamon and apricot are a threesome I cannot resist, and this spicy sweet tagine is bursting with flavour and warmth – and all in one pot.

The healthy riff on traditional couscous packs in some extra plant-based goodness and the sweetness of the parsnip gently complements the tangy, juicy apricot. Don't be afraid to throw on extra herbs, while the optional crunchy pomegranate seeds add some Middle Eastern magic.

Heat the olive oil in a tagine or large cast-iron pot over a medium heat and sauté the onions for about 5 minutes, or until golden. Add the lamb, spices and a sprinkle of salt and cook over a high heat for 5–6 minutes until each cube is browned all over.

Lower the heat and add the chopped tomatoes, stock and another pinch of salt. Cover and simmer over a low heat for 1½–2 hours, stirring regularly and adding more stock or water if needed. Stir in the chopped apricots for the last 30 minutes of cooking time.

Meanwhile, prepare the couscous. Grate the cauliflower and parsnips using a medium grater or food processor with a grater blade. Place in a bowl and add the chilli, cumin, oil, parsley, pomegranate seeds (if using) and salt and pepper. Toss thoroughly, then taste and adjust the seasoning.

Serve with the lamb and an extra sprinkling of chopped parsley.

3 large courgettes

FOR THE PESTO
10 sundried tomatoes
2 tbsp nutritional yeast

1 red pepper, deseeded and chopped
100g macadamia nuts
40g almonds, ideally soaked
　in water for at least 8 hours

5 tbsp olive oil
1 garlic clove
salt and freshly ground black pepper

COURGETTE 'SPAGHETTI' WITH RED PEPPER PESTO

RAW / VEGAN

Serves 3–4

Pasta with pesto was one of the only things I knew how to cook as a student and I still yearn for it almost ten years later. This wholefood version does not disappoint, and the nutritional yeast and macadamia nuts are as good as – or better than – any Parmesan cheese. You can also make this with carrots or butternut squash instead of courgettes, although butternut is trickier to spiralise. If you don't have a spiraliser, a julienne peeler works just as well.

Start by spiralising your courgettes. Once done, place them in a bowl with a little salt and set aside for 5–10 minutes to soften.

Meanwhile, pulse all the pesto ingredients in a food processor or blender until you have a chunky paste; taste and adjust the seasoning.

Gently drain the excess liquid from the courgette, mix with the pesto and serve with freshly ground black pepper.

145g dried chickpeas, soaked and cooked until tender (or 1 × 400g tin, rinsed and drained)
1 medium beetroot, peeled and grated

½ onion
1 garlic clove
1 tsp ground cumin, or to taste
50g unsalted pistachios
2 tbsp olive or coconut oil

a large handful of fresh parsley
1 tbsp buckwheat flour
1 tsp bicarbonate of soda
Tahini Everything Sauce (see page 172), to serve

BEETROOT FALAFEL

VEGAN

Serves 3–4

When I lived in Paris in my early twenties I would trek to the Marais most nights to get my fill of delicious falafel. I wanted to create a version of the staple that was as colourful as it was tasty, and that could be baked or fried. These lend themselves to either method and go perfectly with the Tahini Everything Sauce (see page 172) – falafel and tahini are a combo that cannot be beaten. The buckwheat flour can be a little hard to get hold of but it is worth seeking out. If you have buckwheat groats and a good blender, you can always make your own flour; alternatively use any gluten-free flour, although you won't get the same nuttiness that you get with buckwheat.

Preheat the oven to 200°C/gas 6 and line a baking tray with baking parchment or a non-stick baking sheet.

Tip all the ingredients into a food processor or blender and pulse until a chunky paste forms.

Roll into small balls with your hands, gently flatten them and place on the baking tray. Cover with foil and cook in the oven for 10 minutes. Remove the foil and cook for another 5–6 minutes, until crispy and cooked through. Alternatively, fry in a little olive or coconut oil over a medium-high heat for about 5–6 minutes, turning once.

Serve immediately, with the Tahini Everything Sauce and a crunchy salad.

SALADS
& SIDES

For me, sides and salads are where we can really enjoy a nutritional rainbow, and where I like to incorporate all the fresh herbs and leaves I find at local shops or markets into vibrant, fibre-filled creations. With a delicious sprinkle and a couple of versatile go-to dressings (see pages 172–3) – as well as quick and easy drizzles of olive oil and lemon, or hemp oil and tamari – any raw leaves and veggies can be jazzed up into a tasty plant-based dish. Add a grain for extra bulk and you have a healthy one-plate meal.

It's also fun to forage and get creative with what you use in salads: edible flowers and herbs from the garden for extra flavour and colour (see the Green Bitters Salad with Nigella and Nasturtiums, page 126), fresh or dried fruits for a hint of sweetness (Winter Slaw with Pear and Walnuts, page 119), foraged nettles for organic goodness (page 121) or crunchy roasted seeds for texture… don't be afraid to try new combinations and see what works for you and your family.

It is so important to eat enough fibre each day, both soluble and insoluble, and on a typical western diet this isn't always easy. Fibre performs many important functions so the more salads, leaves and veggies we can eat at each meal, the better. When people start to include more plants in their diet, they often notice immediate changes: with even blood sugar levels and proper elimination, our complexions clear, our eyes shine brighter, our energy levels are more stable and we can fly higher for longer without relying so heavily on stimulants like sugar and coffee to get us through the day. The following recipes will get you started, alongside delicious dips and sauces to keep things fresh and varied.

170g short grain brown rice

2 large handfuls of kale, stems removed, washed and chopped

1 tbsp lemon juice

2 tbsp hemp oil

2 garlic cloves

15 blanched almonds, ideally soaked in water for at least 8 hours

1 tbsp olive or coconut oil

1–2 tbsp tamari, or to taste

½ ripe avocado

salt and freshly ground black pepper

FOR THE PICKLED CARROT

1 small carrot, grated

4 tsp apple cider vinegar

1 tsp coconut palm sugar

KALE & AVOCADO RICE WITH PICKLED CARROT

VEGAN

Serves 2

The nutty short grain rice makes a satisfying counterpart to the raw kale and avocado in this light and delicious salad. The quick-pickled carrot adds some colourful sweetness and if you make double quantities you can keep it in a Kilner jar in the fridge and add it to any salad, along with some Nori Za'atar Sprinkle (see page 175).

Bring a pan of salted water to the boil and add the rice; simmer for 20–30 minutes, or according to the packet instructions. When the rice is tender but still has some bite remove it from the heat, drain and set aside.

Meanwhile, to make the pickle, mix the grated carrot with 3 teaspoons of the apple cider vinegar and the sugar in a bowl and set aside to marinate. In a separate bowl, mix the kale, lemon juice, 1 tablespoon of the hemp oil and a sprinkle of salt and massage gently with your hands for 5 minutes so that the leaves begin to soften; set aside.

Use a pestle and mortar to crush the garlic and almonds to a fine crumble. Heat the olive or coconut oil in a frying pan over a medium heat and gently sauté the almond crumble until brown and crispy. Take care not to burn it as the garlic cooks very quickly.

When the rice is done, mix it with two-thirds of the crumble, the remaining teaspoon of apple cider vinegar and the remaining hemp oil. Season to taste with the tamari.

To serve, pile up the rice, kale and carrot and top with rough scoops of avocado. Garnish with the remaining crumble, a drizzle of hemp oil and tamari and some black pepper.

a handful of walnuts
½ red cabbage, shredded
½ savoy cabbage, shredded
1 pear, cored and thinly sliced

a handful of fresh mint,
  roughly chopped
FOR THE DRESSING
3 tsp Dijon mustard

3 tbsp olive oil
3 tsp apple cider vinegar
salt

WINTER SLAW WITH PEAR & WALNUTS

VEGETARIAN

Serves 2

The warm mustard and hearty savoy make this slaw ideal for the colder months, with the hot kick of Dijon helping to fight off the cold. The classic pairing of pear and walnut is brought to life with fresh mint and the whole thing is so quick to throw together – perfect with a Sunday roast or for a packed lunch on the go.

Lightly toast the walnuts in a dry frying pan over a medium heat for 4–5 minutes, taking care not to burn them. Set aside to cool and then roughly chop.

Place the shredded cabbage, pear and most of the mint in a large bowl. Mix the dressing ingredients together in a glass or jug and toss over the salad, mixing thoroughly and seasoning with salt to taste. Serve sprinkled with the walnuts and remaining mint.

3 large handfuls of chard
1 tbsp hemp oil

1–2 tsp tamari
freshly ground black pepper

TAMARI CHARD

VEGAN

Serves 2

Tamari and hemp oil are such a great match, and this simple recipe is the best way I know to whip up some vitamin-rich chard with minimal time, fuss and effort. Three ingredients and a grinding of black pepper: that's all there is to it.

I like to use chard because of its intense, earthy flavour and amazing rainbow colours; spinach, cavolo nero or spring greens are also delicious, or broccoli for a little more crunch. Tenderstem or purple sprouting are the sweetest and, in my opinion, most delicious. I've served this with the Wild Salmon and Quinoa Cakes on page 100.

Place a large pan over a medium heat until a drop of water steams off it. Add the chard and a splash of water and steam for 2–3 minutes, until cooked through but still tender.

Remove from the heat and dress with the hemp oil and tamari, adjusting to taste. Finish with freshly ground black pepper to serve.

3 red peppers, thickly sliced
olive oil
salt

FOR THE PESTO
a handful of nettles

a handful of fresh basil
a handful of spinach
15 blanched almonds, ideally soaked
    in water for at least 8 hours
5 macadamias

2 tbsp nutritional yeast
juice of ½ lemon
1 small garlic clove
salt and freshly ground black pepper

ROAST PEPPERS WITH NETTLE PESTO

VEGAN

Serves 2–3

Foraging is great fun and such an empowering way to connect to the food you eat and its origins. And nothing is easier to get hold of in our gardens and wild spaces than the humble stinging nettle; with its dark green iron-rich leaves, slightly astringent taste, diuretic properties and abundant benefits for the skin and adrenals, it is a true backyard hero – perfect steeped in tea or whizzed up in this fresh summer pesto with sweet roast peppers.

Nettles are best picked in spring: the top four or five leaves are the ones you want, and any that have started to flower should be avoided. Ideally, you want to gather them away from roads or concentrated pollution – and remember to wear gloves!

Preheat the oven to 180°C/gas 4.

Rub the peppers with a little oil and salt and roast them in a baking tray for 15–20 minutes, until soft and golden.

Meanwhile, pulse all the ingredients for the pesto in a food processor or blender until smooth. Taste and adjust the seasoning.

Serve the peppers warm or at room temperature with the pesto drizzled on top and a sprinkling of freshly ground black pepper. This is a quick and versatile side dish to accompany any meat or veggie dish and makes a lovely healthy addition to summer Sunday roasts.

DIPS

VEGAN

Makes 1
large bowl
of each

Dips are a great way to sneak extra vitamins and nutrients into our mealtimes without even trying. I often serve a generous spoonful of hummus or baba ganoush on the side of my plate or with a salad – or just snack on them during the day using crunchy vegetables or the Omega Seed Crackers (see page 81) to scoop them up. Smoky, creamy and the king of the dip world, baba ganoush has always held a very sacred place in my taste buds and my heart. I love the warm, exotic flavours and the zingy aftertaste of the aubergine, and I always marvel at how simple it is to make versus how much flavour it gives in return. Meanwhile, hummus is often a reliable nourishing staple for many healthy eaters, and any new variation is a welcome addition to our repertoire. I made this vibrant smoky one for a winter supper club and it has since become a firm favourite in the Naturalista kitchen. I particularly like it because you can use tinned chickpeas and ready-cooked, vacuum-packed beetroot – cornershop items that save you time on busy days and come together into a beautiful little bowl of goodness. Both of these will keep for a couple of days, covered, in the fridge.

BABA GANOUSH

2 large aubergines
2 tbsp olive oil
3 tbsp tahini
1 small garlic clove, crushed
juice of ½ lemon
a handful of fresh parsley,
    finely chopped
a small handful of fresh mint,
    chopped
salt and freshly ground black pepper

Stab your aubergines with a knife or fork and char them over a flame on the hob. Keep turning them regularly until the skin is burned all over; remove from the heat and set aside to cool.

When cool, scrape the flesh out of the skins, discarding the core and seeds. Place in a sieve to drain out the excess liquid, then tip into a bowl and mix in the olive oil, tahini, garlic and lemon juice. Season to taste.

Stir in the herbs before serving at room temperature.

SMOKY BEET HUMMUS

230g cooked chickpeas
    (or 1 × 400g tin, drained
    and rinsed)
260g cooked beetroot
2 tbsp tahini
1–2 tsp tamari
1 small garlic clove
juice of ½ large lemon
½ tsp smoked paprika,
    plus extra to garnish
salt and freshly ground black pepper
fresh parsley, to garnish

Place all the ingredients except the parsley in a blender or food processor and blitz until smooth and creamy. Taste and adjust the seasoning.

Spoon into a serving bowl and garnish with parsley and an extra pinch of smoked paprika.

1 tbsp coconut or olive oil
4 large shallots, peeled and
    thinly sliced lengthways
a handful of pumpkin seeds
70g rocket
1 large head of chicory

50g watercress
a big bunch of herbs, roughly
    chopped (parsley, chives,
    coriander)
1 tsp nigella seeds
nasturtium flowers, to garnish

FOR THE DRESSING
1 tbsp apple cider vinegar
1 generous tsp Dijon mustard
3 tbsp cold-pressed olive oil
1 tsp honey
salt and freshly ground black pepper

GREEN BITTERS SALAD WITH NIGELLA & NASTURTIUMS

VEGETARIAN

Serves 2–3

This warm, peppery salad is a wonderful go-to side dish when you need a good dose of greens. Bitter leaves like rocket and chicory are important in the diet as they stimulate digestion in the stomach and promote optimal nutrient breakdown and absorption. The golden shallots and honey cut through the leaves with a gentle sweetness, while nasturtiums and nigella add some fragrant colour and crunch. I tend to use whatever herbs are available, and if you want to add a milder leaf, you can substitute some of the watercress for Little Gem or Cos lettuce.

Heat the oil in a small pan over a medium heat and fry the shallots until soft and crispy around the edges. In a separate dry pan, toast the pumpkin seeds over a low heat for 3–4 minutes, until they are lightly golden. Remove both pans from the heat and set aside to cool.

Mix the rocket, chicory, watercress and herbs together in a salad bowl. To make the dressing, whisk together the vinegar, mustard, oil and honey in a small bowl and season well with salt and pepper.

Dress the salad just before serving and garnish each plate with the crispy shallots, nigella seeds, pumpkin seeds and nasturtium flowers.

1 cauliflower
6 tbsp olive or coconut oil
4 tbsp polenta
2 tbsp nutritional yeast
salt and freshly ground black pepper

a large handful of fresh parsley
a large handful of basil leaves
3 tbsp olive oil
1 tbsp lemon juice

1 small garlic clove
freshly ground black pepper
6 anchovy fillets, in oil (optional)

POLENTA CAULIFLOWER STEAKS WITH SALSA VERDE

Serves 2 as a
main or 4 as
a side

Crunchy, cheesy (from the nutritional yeast) and dairy-free, these cauliflower steaks make every vegan smile. The tangy salsa verde harnesses all the power of English summer herbs. Anchovies provide an optional hit of salty protein but for a vegan version, leave out the anchovies and add a good sprinkle of salt instead.

The salsa is equally good with fish or on leftover veggies, and really comes to life with a good grinding of black pepper.

Preheat the oven to 200°C/gas 6.

First make the salsa verde. Place all the ingredients in a food processor or blender and blitz until smooth. Spoon into a bowl and chill until ready to serve.

Wash and trim your cauliflower and cut it into 2.5cm-thick slices (depending on the size of the cauliflower you will get about 3 or 4 steaks out of it). You will be left with a few florets at the end; keep these as they can roast alongside the steaks.

Place the cauliflower slices in a large baking tray and drizzle all over with 3 tablespoons of the oil. Rub it in so they are all covered, then sprinkle over 2 tablespoons of polenta and 1 tablespoon of nutritional yeast, making sure they are evenly covered. Sprinkle with a little salt, turn the pieces over and repeat.

Roast in the oven for 15 minutes, then turn the cauliflower slices over and return to the oven for a further 5 minutes. It should be crunchy and golden on the outside with a little bite in the middle. Serve with the salsa verde.

1 head of broccoli, broken into florets
2 large handfuls of kale or cavolo
  nero, washed and chopped

FOR THE SAUCE
2 tbsp almond butter
1–2 tsp miso
1 tsp tamari

4–5 tbsp warm water
2 tsp coconut palm sugar
a pinch of chilli flakes

MISO ALMOND GREENS

VEGAN

Serves 2–3

This was a winter staple in the Rainbo van and has become our go-to recipe for jazzing up dark leafy greens and brassicas. Brassicas are often overlooked (and overcooked!) as a boring vegetable but if gently steamed, they are deliciously sweet and crunchy and a brilliant source of hormone-balancing phytoestrogens. And don't throw away their stalks: this is the juicy part where most of the nutrients are stored.

I use white miso, which is a little sweeter than the darker variety, but different brands vary so go slow with it. You can always taste the sauce and add more if you think it needs more salt.

You can keep any leftover sauce in an airtight jar in the fridge for up to 6 days.

Whisk all the sauce ingredients together in a jug until combined. Taste and adjust the flavours as desired.

Lightly steam the greens for 3–4 minutes (you want them still to have some bite). If you like your broccoli on the softer side, steam it in a separate basket for 1–2 minutes longer.

Serve the greens warm with the sauce drizzled over.

a handful of cashews
1 tbsp coconut palm sugar
¼ large red cabbage or ½ small,
  shredded
3 carrots, grated

a handful of fresh coriander,
  roughly chopped
<u>FOR THE DRESSING</u>
2cm piece of fresh ginger,
  finely grated

1 small garlic clove, crushed
1 tbsp mirin
1 tbsp tamari
1 tsp rice vinegar

ASIAN RAINBOW SLAW

VEGAN

Serves 3–4

This bright crunchy slaw is the basis of our signature Rainbo Freedom Box and has been a staple on our menu since we first opened the hatch. It is quick, healthy and moreish and goes with almost everything, from Asian meat and fish to grain-based salads and noodle bowls (see page 97). You can use any herbs you like but fresh coriander is a brilliant place to start.

See the photograph on page 89 where this is served with my Cashew Beef Satay.

Lightly toast the cashews in a dry frying pan over a medium heat until golden. Add the coconut palm sugar and stir quickly into the cashews until it melts into a caramel. It will burn easily so reduce the heat as you do this. Once the cashews are caramelised, remove from the heat and set aside to cool.

Thoroughly combine all the ingredients for the dressing in a blender (or use a pestle and mortar). Combine the shredded cabbage and carrots in a serving bowl and mix in the dressing. Serve topped with the cashews and coriander.

FOOD HERO: GINGER

I love ginger and relish an excuse to throw it in to almost anything I am cooking, if I can. Whether in power balls, sweet energy bars or warming tagines (see pages 62, 74 or 106) and Asian-inspired creations, the root brings a spicy warmth to everything it touches. It is one of the few spices I also like to use on its own – a little chunk in hot water can warm up the chilliest of mornings, both emotionally and physically.

Usually I like to use the fresh root as it has the most flavour and a lovely crunchy texture, but I keep a jar of ground ginger in the cupboard too, for days when I have run out, or just a small sprinkle is needed. The powdered form also goes well with baking and sweeter flavours. The main strength of ginger as a flavour is its versatile heat, and it has been used in Indian and Asian cooking for centuries to harness its sweet and warming properties. It is particularly revered for its benefits to the digestive system, speeding up the metabolism, stimulating digestive enzymes and helping to naturally relieve nausea and stomach upset, including morning, travel and chemotherapy-induced sickness. It also has antispasmodic properties, that can help relieve stomach pain and tension, and can be used as a mild natural laxative if regular bowel function is off track.

Like its root cousin turmeric, ginger is also a rich source of antioxidants and it provides antiviral and antiparasitic properties, making it a useful companion when travelling and when your immunity needs a boost. A few slices in some hot water with honey and lemon is a universal hug in a mug and, with an added dash of cayenne to further boost circulation and heat, a great cold and lurgy fighter.

Its compounds – gingerols – provide broad anti-inflammatory action, and have been shown to suppress the formation of pro-inflammatory compounds called cytokines and chemokines.

Turn to page 71 to read about the benefits of turmeric and page 44 to read about cinnamon.

120g quinoa
1 medium cucumber, diced
3 large tomatoes, diced

4 tbsp olive oil
4 tbsp lemon juice
2 handfuls of fresh parsley

2 handfuls of fresh mint
salt and freshly ground black pepper

QUINOA TABBOULEH

VEGAN

Serves 4–6

This healthy quinoa tabbouleh is so easy and delicious, relying solely on tasty ripe veggies and mountains of fresh herbs for instant fresh summer flavour. I have made it with organic and non-organic vegetables and the difference in taste is always overwhelming: go for organic whenever you can. Don't be afraid to pile on the herbs: they're what bring this dish to life.

The trick here is to not overcook the quinoa. If you do, just squeeze it through some muslin to remove the excess moisture.

Rinse the quinoa thoroughly in cold water. Add to a pan with double the volume of water and bring to the boil. Cover, reduce the heat and simmer for about 15 minutes or so, until the white rings start falling away from the grain but it is still firm with a little bite. Remove from the heat, rinse again, drain and set aside in a large bowl to cool.

Mix the quinoa with the cucumber and tomatoes and dress with the oil and lemon juice, seasoning to taste. Roughly chop the herbs and run them through the mixture just before serving.

No.05
PUDDINGS

Oh, how I love puddings: sometimes a meal just doesn't feel complete without a little hit of sweetness to round things off. My mother brought me up on some life-affirming rice puddings (which I have recreated on page 151) and chocolate mousses (see page 153) and people often freak out at the thought that they need to forego comforts like these on the healthy eating path. Not so: with a little creativity, you can indulge in some delicious treats that keep sugar low and fibre high. My Banoffee Chia Pots (see page 147) and Raw Acai and Blueberry Cheesecake (see page 141) are nutritious wholefood riffs on after-dinner classics, while the vibrant green spirulina cacao dip (see page 144) revives most people's love of fruit: whole punnets of strawberries and chopped apples vanish in a matter of minutes.

One thing I recommend to all age groups is to try and eat fresh fruit for pudding or a snack at least twice a week. It can be hard in the UK where we do not have a perennial abundance of juicy peaches and papaya, but dusting some seasonal apples and pears with a little maca and cacao, or roasting strawberries and rhubarb with a light coating of vanilla bean paste makes a delicious healthy pudding full of vitamins and goodness. I have found through trial and error that a well-stocked pantry is key for impromptu bursts of pudding creativity – and when they happen you want to be able to really let rip.

FOR THE BASE
55g pecans
60g dates (look for the
    Deglet Nour variety)
a pinch of salt

FOR THE TOPPING
120g cashews, soaked in water
    for 1 hour
125g frozen blueberries
grated zest of ½ lemon

juice of 1 lemon
1 tbsp acai powder, plus extra to serve
3 tbsp honey
4 tbsp coconut oil
1 tsp vanilla bean paste

RAW ACAI & BLUEBERRY 'CHEESECAKE'

RAW / VEGETARIAN

Serves 6

I don't know many people, young or fully-grown, who don't go weak at the knees for a slice of cheesecake. With creamy cashews and a salty pecan base, this acai and blueberry version is one of my favourite nutritional riffs on the classic treat and the beautiful colour brings a little dose of wonder and awe to any pudding situation.

This works best in a round loose-bottomed cake tin, about 15–18cm in diameter. If you don't have one, simply line a baking dish with cling film and gently pull it out when set.

Blitz the pecans, dates and salt in a food processor until they form a sticky dough when compacted. Transfer to your cake tin or lined dish and press down to make a base. Place in the freezer to set while you make the topping.

Drain the cashews and then place in a food processor or blender with the remaining ingredients and blitz until smooth and creamy, adjusting the sweetness with more honey to taste. Spoon on top of the base and return to the freezer to set for at least 1 hour.

Remove from the freezer and place in the fridge to thaw about 20 minutes before serving. Finish with a sprinkle of acai powder before cutting into slices and serving chilled.

800g fresh fruit, chopped

a handful of fresh basil,
   finely chopped

a handful of fresh mint,
   finely chopped

½ large ripe avocado, stoned
   and peeled

1 apple, peeled, cored and
   cut into small chunks

5 strawberries, hulled

1 tbsp spirulina powder

3 tbsp cacao powder

1 tbsp nut butter

2 tbsp honey

HERBED FRUIT SALAD WITH SPIRULINA CACAO DIP

RAW / VEGETARIAN

Serves 4

The protein- and vitamin-dense spirulina gives this raw chocolatey dip a fabulous dark green colour, which intrigues kids and adults alike, while the super-fresh fruit perfectly harnesses the taste of summer. Use whatever fruit you like – those that are in season are best – to create endless possibilities of flavour and colour. My ideal combination is something like strawberries, pineapple, apple, nectarine, banana and passion fruit. You can also switch up the herbs but this cool combination of basil and mint is a lovely pairing.

First make the dip. Place all the ingredients in a food processor or blender and blitz until smooth and creamy. Cover and chill in the fridge until you are ready to serve.

Place the chopped fruit in a bowl and add the herbs. Toss together and serve with the dip.

60g sour dried cherries
100g cacao butter
70g honey
a pinch of salt

90g cacao powder
coconut palm sugar, to dust
   (optional)

SOUR CHERRY CHOCOLATES

RAW / VEGETARIAN

Makes about
10 chocolates

Rich, dark, sour and sweet, these raw cherry chocolates are the real deal. The decadent cherries cut perfectly through the buttery cacao and there is just enough honey to keep the sweeter-toothed among us satisfied. These work best if you can find dried cherries that are soft and sticky – they have a real bite to them and a moreish, chewy texture. I have kept the honey on the minimal side – you can taste as you go and add more if you want. I usually use a chocolate mould but if you do not have one you can just as easily make chocolate bark by pouring the mixture into a baking tray.

If you are using a chocolate mould, start by placing a cherry in each mould. If you are making bark, line a baking tray with non-stick baking parchment.

Melt the cacao butter in a heatproof glass bowl set over a pan of simmering water (make sure the bottom of the bowl doesn't touch the water). When it is all melted stir in the honey, salt and cacao powder and remove from the heat when thoroughly mixed.

Pour into the mould and place in the fridge for 20 minutes to set. If you are making bark, pour onto the lined baking tray, spread out in an even layer and scatter the cherries over the top before chilling in the fridge.

Store in the fridge for up to 7 days and dust with coconut palm sugar before serving, if you like.

12 large dates (look for the
  Deglet Nour variety)
75g desiccated coconut
a pinch of salt

100g chia seeds
5 ripe bananas
1 × 400g tin coconut milk
1 tsp vanilla bean paste

juice of 1 lemon
1 tbsp maple syrup
1 tsp coconut oil
desiccated coconut and black sesame
  seeds, to sprinkle

BANOFFEE CHIA POTS

VEGAN

Serves 4–6

I have loved banoffee pie since I can remember (does anyone not?) but condensed milk and whipped canned cream leave me down and out for the rest of the day. This light and fluffy chia version, with coconut and sesame for a little eastern flavour, is the perfect healthy alternative and super quick to whip up. The kids will go crazy for it too.

First make the base. Blitz the dates, coconut and a generous pinch of salt in a food processor until a sticky mixture forms. Divide between tumblers and press down firmly, then place in the fridge to set while you make the pudding.

Place the chia seeds, 4 of the bananas, coconut milk, vanilla bean paste, lemon juice and maple syrup in a food processor or blender and blitz until smooth. Distribute evenly between the glasses and return to the fridge to set.

Slice the remaining banana diagonally while you melt the coconut oil in a small pan over a medium heat. Sauté the banana slices for a few minutes until golden on both sides. Top each pudding with the banana slices and serve sprinkled with desiccated coconut and black sesame seeds.

FOR THE BASE
125g dried chickpeas, soaked
in water overnight and boiled
for 45 minutes until soft
(or 1 × 400g tin, drained)
120g almond butter
4 tbsp maple syrup

2 tsp vanilla bean paste
2 tsp ground cinnamon
½ tsp sea salt
¼ tsp baking powder
¼ tsp bicarbonate of soda
FOR THE ICING
1 ripe avocado, stoned and peeled

3 tbsp coconut oil
7 large dates, (look for the
Deglet Nour variety)
3 tbsp cacao powder
1 tbsp maple syrup
a pinch of sea salt
ground cinnamon, to sprinkle

CHICKPEA BLONDIES WITH CACAO AVOCADO ICING

VEGAN

Makes 20

The humble chickpea meets a noble fate in these easy and delicious flourless chickpea blondies. Packed full of iron, potassium, vitamin B6 and magnesium, they're a super-healthy alternative to their dairy- and gluten-laden cousins and one of the most popular recipes from my blog. The cacao avocado icing adds some rich chocolatey creaminess to this plant-based teatime treat and they're a great way to sneak some healthy protein into the kids' diets without so much as a raised eyebrow. Served with juicy strawberries and sprinkled with cinnamon, they don't hang around for long.

Preheat the oven to 170°C/gas 3 ½ and grease or line a 28 × 19cm baking tray with baking parchment.

If you're using tinned chickpeas, rinse them thoroughly first. Place the chickpeas in a food processor along with the remaining ingredients for the base and pulse until the mixture is a thick doughy consistency. Taste and add more salt, maple syrup or cinnamon if desired.

Pour the mixture into the prepared baking tray and bake for 17–20 minutes, watching closely towards the end. They're ready when they are a little golden on top and you can stick a knife in and bring it out clean, but you want to keep them on the soft side. Remove from the oven and leave to cool in the tin while you prepare the icing (this is best spread on just before serving).

Place all the ingredients for the icing, except the ground cinnamon, in a food processor or a blender and blitz until smooth and creamy. When ready to serve, spread over the top of the blondie, sprinkle with cinnamon and cut into squares. Serve with fresh fruit.

Both the blondie and icing can be made a day ahead and kept, covered, in the fridge.

160g black rice, soaked for
4–8 hours in water
1 × 400g tin coconut milk

½ tsp sea salt
4–5 tbsp coconut palm sugar
a splash unsweetened nut milk

1 ripe mango, peeled and diced

BLACK COCONUT RICE WITH MANGO

VEGAN

Serves 2–3

The exotic flavours of this recipe instantly transport me to the warm shores of Southeast Asia and this recipe is one of my favourite versions of that all-time classic: rice pudding. Black rice has such a lovely, nutty texture and looks beautiful with the bright and vibrant mango. Banana and pineapple also work well, and the dusting of coconut palm sugar is essential for that salty-sweet butterscotchy deliciousness.

Place the drained rice, coconut milk and salt in a medium non-stick pan. Bring to the boil then simmer gently over a low heat for 45 minutes, or until the rice is soft and creamy but still has some bite. You may need to add a little water as it cooks. Stir frequently to keep the rice well mixed and make sure it doesn't stick to the bottom.

When it is cooked, mix in 3 tablespoons of the coconut palm sugar (or more to taste). Remove from the heat and serve in a bowl with a splash of nut milk, the diced mango and the remaining sugar sprinkled on top.

1 ripe medium avocado
4 tbsp cacao powder
2 tbsp honey or maple syrup

1 tbsp nut butter
2 tbsp coconut oil
a pinch of salt

optional flavourings: ground
   cinnamon, orange oil, coffee
   or maca, mint oil or leaves

2-MINUTE CACAO AVOCADO MOUSSE

RAW / VEGETARIAN

Serves 4

Shop-bought chocolate is one of the hardest things to say goodbye to on the clean eating path, and as a lifelong chocoholic, I spend most of my time concocting healthy cacao-based alternatives. Once you experience the magic of raw cacao, you will neither want nor need to go back, and this quick little mousse perfectly harnesses its flavour and nutrients with minimal planning or effort. At home we call it emergency choc mousse – you'd be amazed how often it's needed, and how quickly it banishes the blues.

This is a good base recipe and depending on the season or your mood you can add a little extra warmth with a couple of drops of orange oil and a dash of ground cinnamon, or a drop or two of cooling peppermint oil and some young fresh mint leaves as a garnish. Coconut aficionados can also add a teaspoon or two of desiccated flakes for extra flavour, and sometimes I like to incorporate a pinch of maca or ground coffee for a little mocha flavoured after-dinner pick-me-up. Once you master the basics, you can play around with variations according to what's in the cupboard and customise it with your favourite extras.

Halve the avocado and remove the stone, then scoop the flesh into a food processor or blender. Add the remaining ingredients, including any optional flavourings, and blend on high speed until smooth.

Spoon into ramekins or small bowls and chill in the fridge for 10 minutes before serving.

3 large bananas, peeled,
cut into chunks and frozen
cacao nibs and coconut palm
sugar, to sprinkle

FOR THE COCONUT CHOC SAUCE
3 tbsp coconut oil
2 tbsp maple syrup
4 tbsp cacao powder

PURE BANANA ICE CREAM WITH COCONUT CHOC SAUCE

VEGAN

Serves 4

The richness of this pure banana ice cream defies its simple ingredients; it is an instant hit whenever I serve it and no one can believe it doesn't contain dairy. The cacao coconut sauce goes deliciously crunchy on top, and the bitter nibs and butterscotchy coconut palm sugar are a match made in heaven.

This works best in a Vitamix but any high-speed blender will do – just go very slowly and thaw the banana a little more to soften it before you liquidise it. The ice cream is best served immediately.

Remove the banana chunks from the freezer and thaw for 5 minutes (a little longer if not using a Vitamix) before blending until creamy. Start slowly and increase the speed gradually as they soften. Divide between bowls and place in the fridge while you prepare the sauce.

Melt the coconut oil in a small pan and stir in the maple syrup and cacao powder. After about a couple of minutes, when everything is thoroughly mixed together, pour it over the ice cream. Sprinkle with the cacao nibs and coconut palm sugar and serve immediately.

40g cacao butter
35g coconut oil
3 tbsp honey
5 tbsp cacao powder,
plus extra to dust

1 tbsp finely grated fresh ginger
2 tbsp finely grated orange zest
1 tbsp orange juice
1½ tsp ground cinnamon,
plus extra to dust (optional)

½ tsp ground ginger
5 cloves, crushed with
    a pestle and mortar
a pinch of salt

CHRISTMAS TRUFFLES

VEGETARIAN

Makes 10
truffles

For me, Christmas has such a distinctive taste, full of spices and warmth and merriment, and these healthy little truffles are a deliciously rich and chocolatey homage to all that I love about the winter holidays. Fragrant cloves and spicy ginger combine with orange and cacao in a decadent plant-based mixture of buttery indulgence. Give them to guests as a treat or gift and they will be surprised to learn that they aren't laden with double cream.

The inclusion of ground ginger alongside the fresh gives a deeper flavour but isn't absolutely vital, and you can add more cloves and cinnamon if you like things a little spicier. In fact, there's never been a better recipe to try as you go. And you might want to make double quantities, as in my experience they are quite difficult to say no to.

Place the cacao butter and coconut oil in a heatproof bowl and set over a pan of barely simmering water until melted (make sure the bottom of the bowl doesn't touch the water). Remove from the heat, add the honey and whisk well until thoroughly mixed.

Add the cacao powder, fresh ginger, orange zest and juice, mixing thoroughly again before adding the ground spices and salt. Adjust any flavours to taste then place the mixture in the fridge for 10–15 minutes to set. It should form a buttery consistency.

Roll into balls and dust with a little cacao powder and/or ground cinnamon before serving, chilled. Store in an airtight container in the fridge for up to 3 days.

No.06

EVERYDAY
ESSENTIALS

These are the little health food heroes that keep us on the clean eating path day in, day out. Often, in spite of our best efforts to eat well, there can be a dramatic oscillation between moments of passionate inspiration when we fill up the fridge and make beautiful healthy recipes all weekend; and waking up on greyer days with an empty kitchen, leading us to grab a croissant on the way to the Tube and buy any old sandwich for lunch. This chapter is full of the essentials that keep us on the wholefoods and out of the dreaded empty-pantry no man's land. Investing a little time in keeping these flexible friends well stocked at home (and even at work) means we are less likely to resort to processed alternatives and all the nasty ingredients they come with. Sauerkraut (see page 177) is one of the most beneficial foods you can eat, and if you use red cabbage it can be unimaginably beautiful; stocks (page 178) are packed with nutrients and are so easy to prepare; Chia Berry Compote (see page 167) takes minutes to make and is as delicious as it is versatile; Tahini Everything Sauce (see page 172) goes with almost every vegetable known to man... these staples find a way of creeping into almost every breakfast, lunch or dinner. The Everyday Courgette Bread (see page 162) is the result of many free-from baking trials and can go both sweet or savoury depending on how you're feeling, and having a loaf at hand means supermarket alternatives are never a temptation. My troupe of essentials is always evolving, and one is usually hot favourite in our kitchen at any one time. The more you can incorporate these into your cooking routine, the easier it will be to eat healthily, every day.

My mantras are many but one always rings loud and clear: never, ever, run out of stock or Nori Za'atar Sprinkle (see page 175).

165g ground almonds
heaped ½ tsp bicarbonate of soda
a pinch of salt
30g gluten-free oats, ground in
   a food processor or blender

3 eggs, beaten
180g courgettes, coarsely
   grated and squeezed
1 tbsp coconut oil, plus extra
   for greasing

1 tbsp chia seeds
optional flavourings: 1 tbsp
   nutritional yeast or honey or herbs

EVERYDAY COURGETTE BREAD

VEGETARIAN

Makes 1
small loaf

A great gluten-free bread is the toughest challenge for any nutritional cook and to say this recipe was a long time coming is something of an understatement. I like a loaf that isn't based solely on nuts and seeds, and the addition of egg and courgette here keep it healthy and satisfying without being too heavy. The ground almonds have a slightly sweet taste, which goes well with honey if you opt to add it here, but I usually add a little nutritional yeast for a cheesier, more savoury flavour. Play around and see what additions work best for you and your family.

The squeezing of the courgette is vital and not to be skipped! I use a nut milk bag but you can use a clean muslin cloth or tea towel if you don't have one.

Preheat the oven to 180°C/gas 4 and grease a 900g loaf tin with some coconut oil.

In a large bowl, mix together the ground almonds, bicarbonate of soda, salt and ground oats. Add the eggs, grated courgette and coconut oil and mix thoroughly. Finally stir in the chia seeds and any optional flavourings.

Pour into the prepared loaf tin and bake for 40–45 minutes, until the loaf is brown on top and a knife comes out clean when inserted into the middle.

Remove from the tin and leave to cool for 1 hour before slicing and serving. Store in the fridge for up to 3 days in an airtight container or wrapped in cling film.

120g almonds, soaked in water
   overnight
1 litre water

1 tsp coconut oil
3 drops of vanilla extract or the
   seeds from 1 vanilla pod

a pinch of salt
3–4 dates, or 1 tbsp honey or
   syrup, to sweeten (optional)

NUT MILK

RAW / VEGAN

Makes 1 litre

A good nut milk can be one of the most delicious things in the world and learning to make my own has been such an empowering undertaking. The shop-bought options are getting better and better but the majority are not organic, usually undergo a degree of heat processing and contain added refined sugar and salt. It's surprisingly quick to make, and in doing so you can choose where the nuts are sourced so you can be sure you are getting the maximum nutrients with minimal additives. You can use this nut milk in any of the recipes in the book.

You need a high-speed blender for this and can use muslin or a nut milk bag to strain it. The latter is specifically designed for this purpose and well worth investing in.

You can use almost any seed or nut you like; simply blend with water, coconut oil, vanilla and salt. I generally use almonds, and I keep the pulp for a face scrub or to add extra bulk to a cracker mix. Soaking the nuts the night before will increase your body's ability to absorb essential minerals, although cashews, sesame seeds and hemp seeds do not need soaking or straining. If you're short on time or out of almonds, substituting them with cashews makes a quick, easy and deliciously creamy milk – although it separates a little more easily and is not as silky smooth as the strained versions.

Dates – or honey for non-vegans – add the option of sweetness, and you can vary the nuts you use to keep things fresh and inspiring.

Drain the soaked almonds and then add to a blender with the water. Blitz on high speed until they are completely broken down and the water has become creamy. Strain the mixture through muslin or using a nut milk bag to remove the nut pulp.

Return the liquid to the blender and add the coconut oil, vanilla, salt and sweetener. Blend again on the highest speed, pour into a bottle and chill in the fridge for at least 30 minutes before serving. Separation is normal, just shake before use.

Store in the fridge for up to 3 days and use as you would regular milk – in hot drinks, on cereal or as a drink.

125g blueberries
125g raspberries

2 tbsp maple syrup or coconut palm sugar

½ tsp vanilla bean paste
2 tbsp chia seeds

CHIA BERRY COMPOTE

VEGAN

Serves 4–6 with pancakes

This clever instant compote is packed with antioxidants, protein and fibre and is so quick and easy to make you will wonder how you ever managed without it. Add to puddings, fruit, toast or pancakes (see page 41) – or just have a sneaky spoonful when you need perking up.

Place the berries and maple syrup or coconut palm sugar in a pan and bring to the boil over a medium heat. Reduce the heat and simmer for 5 minutes, until the berries are soft.

Remove from the heat and mash to a pulp. Stir in the vanilla and chia seeds and place in a bowl in the fridge to set for 20–30 minutes before serving. Store in an airtight jar in the fridge for up to 1 week.

200g cashews
2 tbsp lemon juice

130ml water
a sprinkle of salt

CASHEW CREAM CHEESE

RAW / VEGAN

Makes 1 small bowl

When eliminating dairy from the diet, the thing most people miss more than anything is some form of cheese. This simple cashew version is a satisfying substitute to cream cheese and can be whipped up instantaneously and used as a sauce, spread or topping for a variety of dishes. It makes a lovely béchamel replacement in the Raw Courgette Lasagne (see page 92) and is also delicious spread on bread with a little Chia Berry Compote (see page 167). Whenever I make a batch I discover yet another use for it.

You will see that the texture and taste evolve as time goes by, and its neutral flavour means it can be added to sweet and savoury dishes with equal ease. If you're going down the savoury route, you can run through a tablespoonful of dried herbs like chives, parsley, dill or thyme and a pinch of powdered garlic, cayenne pepper or nutritional yeast for extra depth and flavour. Fresh herbs are also wonderful but decrease the shelf life to 1 day.

Place all the ingredients in a food processor or blender and blitz on high speed until smooth and creamy, adding more water if you would like it to have a creamier consistency.

Transfer to a bowl, cover and store in the fridge for up to 3–4 days.

EVERYDAY ESSENTIALS

4 tbsp tahini
1 small garlic clove
150ml water

juice of ½ lemon
¼ tsp salt (or more to taste)

TAHINI EVERYTHING SAUCE

RAW / VEGAN

Makes 1 jug

Ben and I once spent many weeks in the kitchen at a retreat centre in Costa Rica and the first thing we learned to make was this delicious sauce, which can be served by the spoonful with pretty much anything: salad, bread, falafel (see page 110), veggie burgers – it is a staple at every meal.

Tahini is a rich source of calcium, while antibacterial garlic helps keep bugs of all kinds at bay. We were never given a recipe, and taught to judge it by sight and taste; I encourage you to do the same, as everyone likes it a little different.

Place all the ingredients in a food processor or blender and blitz until smooth. Taste and adjust the seasoning, adding more tahini, lemon juice or salt as desired.

This recipe can easily be halved, doubled or tripled and will keep in the fridge in an airtight container for up to 1 week.

1 courgette
1 tbsp apple cider vinegar
juice of ½ lemon

2 tbsp olive oil
3 tbsp hemp oil
thumb-sized piece of fresh ginger

1 date (look for the
  Deglet Nour variety)
a pinch of cayenne pepper

CREAMY HERB SALAD DRESSING

RAW / VEGAN

Makes 1 jug

This creamy courgette dressing is brilliantly versatile and perks up any green salad – drizzle over a handful of green leaves, a few scoops of ripe avocado and some seeds to transform something from the mundane to the sublime. Diego Castro taught me the basics and the zingy apple cider vinegar and lemon juice are perfectly balanced by the almost imperceptible sweetness of the date, while cayenne and ginger add a hot little kick.

I like to make a batch and keep it in the fridge for last-minute weekday lunches.

Place all the ingredients in a food processor or blender and blitz until smooth and creamy.

Store in the fridge in an airtight container for up to 3 days.

2 tbsp shredded nori sheets
1 tbsp toasted sesame seeds
¼ tsp salt

½ tsp sumac
½ tsp dried thyme leaves

NORI ZA'ATAR SPRINKLE

RAW / VEGAN

Makes
10 servings

A good salad sprinkle is essential for healthy lunches on the move (and at home). This one will jazz up any salad, rice or quinoa dish or simple avocado on toast, wherever you might find yourself. The dried seaweed is full of essential minerals, including an abundance of iodine, vital for healthy thyroid function and often lacking in the western diet. The zesty sumac and nutty sesame add some delicious depth and flavour.

The recipe below can be doubled or tripled and if you keep some in your bag you will never be far away from a sprinkling of nutrition and flavour. I use dried homegrown thyme from the garden and the young leaves are wonderfully delicate and full of flavour. Some shop-bought mixes can be a little coarser so always go for the greenest, leafiest option.

Mix all the ingredients together and store in an airtight container, jar or tin. It will keep well for up to 3 months if kept dry and out of direct sunlight.

2 medium cabbages
3 tbsp salt

BASIC
SAUERKRAUT

RAW / VEGAN

Makes 1
large jar

Like all fermented foods, sauerkraut is wonderfully beneficial for our gut bacteria and overall health and wellbeing – and a lot cheaper than costly probiotic supplements. Many people think it is hard to make but all it requires is a little patience; the rest is unthinkably easy.

Fermentation is a great way to use up old veggies and also to incorporate vibrant colour into any meal – all you need is one vegetable, salt and some time. Red cabbage becomes the most amazing fuchsia, which brings some flair and beauty to any lunchtime plate.

You'll need a large, sterilised mason jar, plus a sterilised saucer or plate that fits into the neck of the jar (or a ziplock freezer bag).

Core and shred the cabbages and add to a large bowl with the salt. Use you hands to massage the salt into the cabbage; this will help to break down the fibres and soften the cabbage. Once it is malleable and getting juicy, pack it tightly into a sterilised jar. You want to release all the air bubbles; pounding it with the end of a rolling pin or similar object can help pack it in more tightly. Carry on until the cabbage is completely covered in liquid. If there is not enough liquid, make a brine with roughly 1 teaspoon of salt and 250ml water and use to top it up.

Place a sterilised saucer (one that will fit inside the jar) on top of the cabbage and weight it down with something like a glass bottle of water. If you do not have a suitable saucer, use a large ziplock freezer bag filled with water. Cover with a cloth so that it is protected from insects and dust but air can still escape, and store at room temperature. Press down every few hours throughout the first day; as the cabbage softens and releases its water it will become more submerged.

Leave to ferment for 3–4 days, then have a taste and see if you think it is ready. It starts off sharp and tangy and the flavour deepens over time; you may wish to stop the fermentation after a few days or continue to ferment it for longer. Tasting a little each day is a good way to chart its progress and see which flavour you prefer. If you see a foamy looking layer on the surface, just scrape off as much as you can. This is a normal part of the fermentation process.

When you are happy with the flavour, transfer to an airtight container and store in the fridge for up to 2 months.

HOMEMADE STOCK

Makes around 1 litre

A good veg stock is loaded with vitamins and is a kitchen essential for instant vegan plant-based flavour. It is also much easier and quicker to make than most people think. And for those who eat meat, the addition of chicken to the pot provides a rich source of calcium and collagen, which helps repair the effects of gut inflammation and keep membranes healthy.

I like to pour my broths into ice-cube trays and freeze them, so that I have easy access to small amounts when cooking. I usually leave salt until afterwards, depending on what I am making; that way the stock is neutral in flavour, as well as being low in sodium, and therefore child-friendly, but you can add it to the pot if you prefer.

My mother taught me the trick of leaving the skin on the onion for a rich brown colour – it makes all the difference.

VEGETABLE STOCK

VEGAN

2 celery sticks
4 carrots
3 unpeeled onions, halved
10 peppercorns
3 bay leaves
a handful of fresh parsley
a sprig of fresh thyme
1.6 litres cold water

Place all the ingredients in a large pan and bring to the boil. Cover and simmer over a high heat for 40 minutes.

Remove from the heat and allow to cool slightly before straining through muslin or a fine-mesh sieve.

When completely cool store in the fridge for up to 5 days or pour into ice-cube trays and freeze for up to 3 months.

CHICKEN STOCK

1 chicken carcass
   (raw from the butcher or cooked)
1 large unpeeled onion, halved
2 celery sticks
10 peppercorns
5 bay leaves
3–4 sprigs of fresh thyme
1.6 litres cold water

Place all the ingredients in a large pan and bring to the boil. Cover and simmer over a low-medium heat for 3–4 hours. Alternatively place in a very low oven (80°C/gas ¼) for 6–7 hours.

Allow to cool slightly before straining through muslin or a fine-mesh sieve.

When completely cool store in the fridge for up to 5 days or pour into ice-cube trays and freeze for up to 3 months.

HERBAL TEA BLENDS

Makes
1 pot

Herbal teas are a wonderful way to up your micronutrient intake, improve your mood, support the body's natural cycles and increase your hydration. The incredible healing power of herbs and spices is an invaluable wellness aid and the options for customised combinations are almost infinite.

You can buy a varied selection of dried herbs at many health food and holistic shops, while many of the most potent ones grow in our own gardens: basil, mint, rosemary, sage, lavender, verbena and chamomile are all easily grown and dried and provide amazing benefits in fresh infusions.

These everyday blends are easily put together and a good place to start. I use an infuser teapot but you can also brew them in a cafetière; simply fill with boiling water, leave for 5 minutes, plunge and pour. The longer you wait before plunging, the stronger the infusion will become and you might like to sweeten it with a little honey. If using a larger cafetière, you may also want to double the quantities.

AFTER DINNER: LIQUORICE, PEPPERMINT, FENNEL

1 liquorice stick
a generous sprig of fresh mint
1 tsp fennel seeds, lightly crushed with a pestle and mortar

WELL WOMAN: ROSE, CHAMOMILE, RASPBERRY LEAF, ORANGE PEEL

1 tsp dried rose leaves
2 tsp dried chamomile flowers
1 tsp dried raspberry leaves
2 slices of fresh or dried orange peel

DEEP SLEEP: LEMON BALM, CHAMOMILE, LAVENDER

1 tsp fresh lemon balm leaves
2 tsp dried chamomile flowers
½ tsp dried lavender, or to taste

WINTER WARMER: CINNAMON, APPLE PEEL, VANILLA, CARDAMOM

1 cinnamon stick
2 pieces of apple peel (fresh or dried)
1 small vanilla pod
seeds from 5 cardamom pods (crush with a pestle and mortar), or to taste

Part 2

BEAUTY

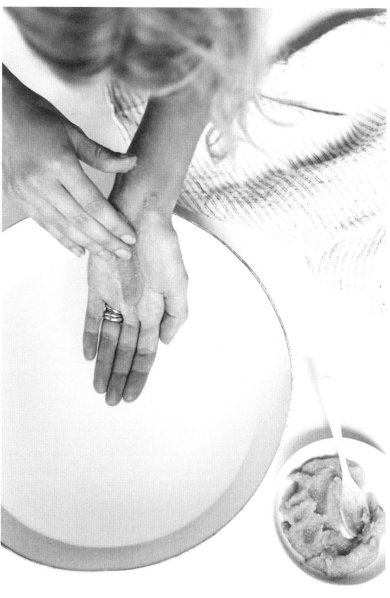

I felt such a unique excitement and pride when I first made my own beauty products. There are so many ingredients in the kitchen that can have real benefits for our skin and hair, and learning to harness their goodness has been a fundamental part of my naturopathic journey. We need to raise our collective and individual awareness of what we put onto our bodies, not just into them, and there has never been a more important time to question what is in the shop-bought lotions we use day in, day out. The nourishing recipes in this chapter offer natural alternatives to those mainstream brands that often contain unwanted chemicals, and, for the most part, they can be made from your kitchen cupboards. Some are bathroom staples; others luxurious treats, and the natural beauty heroes that you'll find throughout the chapter are stand-alone superstar ingredients. Since everyone's body, skin, hair and scalp are different, these are just some ideas to get you started. My own journey in both the bathroom and the kitchen has been an organic one, born of curiosity and trial and error, which I encourage you to follow. Feel your way around which ingredients and uses you want to incorporate into daily life, and if you feel the urge to add another component or try a different method, go for it. Many can also be customised with your favourite essential oils, so that each time you make them they become a little more special and a little more your own.

3 tbsp shea butter
3 tbsp coconut oil
3 tbsp arrowroot powder

3 tbsp bicarbonate of soda
15 drops of essential oil
   (see below for suggestions)

NATURAL
DEODORANT

RAW / VEGAN

Makes 1 jar
or enough for
1–2 months

Since I first made this, there has always been at least one pot on the go in our house and we have hardly used a shop-bought deodorant since. The latter, in its many forms, is usually filled with the kinds of harmful chemicals and compounds that I try to avoid. Aluminium, the main ingredient in most antiperspirants, is not an element we want too much of in our bodies. There is research to suggest that aluminium may be absorbed by the skin and deposited in our tissues, putting strain on our systems as we try to break it down and get it out. And even if you are avoiding antiperspirants altogether and opting for deodorants, the cheap, mass-produced ones often contain parabens and other processed chemicals that our bodies do not know how to safely eliminate. Some research suggests that both aluminium-based compounds and parabens can trigger the production of oestrogen, the hormone responsible for the growth of breast cancer cells, and the number of parabens banned for cosmetic use by the EU is steadily increasing. Finding a natural alternative that doesn't cost a fortune and contains ingredients I recognise and have sourced myself is the only way I can know exactly what I am putting on my skin every day.

This homemade cream is moisturising, effective and simple. It won't stop you really sweating things out if you need to, but it will keep you fresh, clean and smelling of lavender fields. I use a mixture of tea tree and lavender but any essential oils will work, depending on your own preferences (see pages 238–41). Woodier fragrances such as sandalwood with bergamot or orange flower can persuade even the manliest man, while fresher flavours like peppermint and tea tree (particularly great here as it is antibacterial) keep things light and airy.

In a bowl, mix the shea butter and coconut oil together with a fork until it has a smooth and creamy consistency with no lumps. Stir in the arrowroot and bicarbonate of soda and mix thoroughly until you have a thick but malleable paste. You may want to add more arrowroot for thickness, or coconut oil for creaminess.

Mix in the essential oils and store in a non-plastic container at room temperature (or in the fridge if you live in a very warm place). Apply a small amount under arms each morning or when needed.

Used daily, this will last about 2 months (or 1 if sharing with a partner), but will keep for up to 6 months.

200g coconut oil
70g Himalayan pink salt (or more or less, depending on preference)

10–15 drops of cardamom essential oil, or the seeds from 6 cardamom pods, crushed

PINK HIMALAYAN BODY SCRUB

RAW / VEGAN

Makes 8–10 applications

This is one of my favourite skincare recipes because it is so simple to make and it smells like pure holiday. Whenever I make it in workshops people swoon at the heady coconut and cardamom combination and beautiful peachy colour; nothing perks up a cold winter evening quite like it. The pink salt is full of essential macro- and micro-minerals (which we can absorb through the pores) and gently exfoliates dead skin, while the coconut oil locks moisture in and keeps skin soft and supple. I use this once or twice a week all year round.

It lasts forever and also makes a beautiful present: collect small glass jars, fill a few up and you will never be short of some handmade love to give.

Mix all the ingredients together with a fork in a small bowl until they are well combined.

Transfer to a bowl or jar and store at room temperature. To use, apply the scrub to damp skin in the bath or shower, rinse the salt off and gently pat skin dry with a towel. Rinse the bath afterwards to remove any oily residue.

Keeps for up to 12 months.

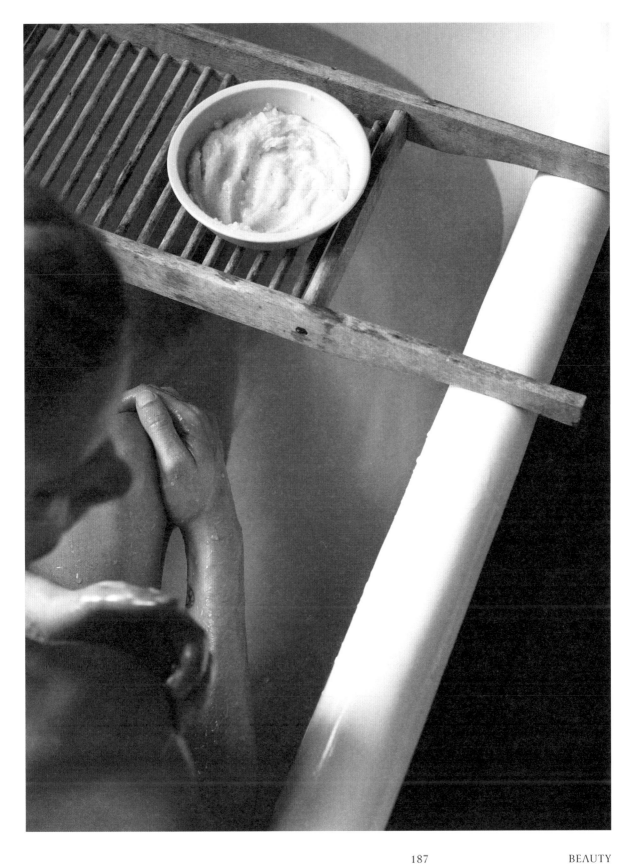

NATURAL BEAUTY HERO: ALOE VERA

Aloe vera (*aloe barbadensis*) is an amazing little plant and one we can all grow in our homes, wherever we live, as long as we have some sunlight. It requires minimal care and delivers amazing benefits in return: its clear, nutrient-filled gel is a brilliant natural skincare aid, densely packed with some 18 amino acids, 12 vitamins and 20 minerals. It also contains high levels of beneficial compounds called polyphenols, which are rich in antioxidants and help treat inflammation. Just as with dietary antioxidants, they mop up free radicals and can help reverse the damaging effects of oxidation on the skin.

You can buy the gel from many health food stores and online, but growing your own means it is fully organic and if it reaches a large enough size you can use it (or a few plants) for the whole family. The leaves can be broken off, peeled and used for a number of natural beauty benefits: the more I harvest its rich transparent gel, the more uses I seem to find for it.

The leaves do not grow back so you want to pick smaller ones for the little jobs and save the bigger ones for larger needs like all over moisturisation or shaving. Pick the leaf from the base of the plant, hold it at an angle for 30 seconds or so to drain the yellow liquid (called aloin) from inside it, then gently peel off the skin with a serrated knife, and remove the transparent gel fillet. This is where the goodness lies and it can be mashed (or blended in larger quantities) to form a paste and used immediately, or stored in cubes in the freezer for emergency sunburn relief. Kept in the fridge, it will last for about 1 week.

MOISTURISER

Aloe's jelly-like texture and high water content make it a gentle, refreshing moisturiser and great for the treatment of mild sunburn and mild skin irritation in both adults and children. Applied to heat rashes and scrapes, it forms a gentle protective layer on the skin and its immune-boosting polysaccharides promote cell regeneration and healing.
– DIRECTIONS: mash or blend the gel and apply a thin layer to the desired area twice daily. It can be cooled and stored in the fridge; you can also add one drop of a cooling essential oil such as peppermint or tea tree for extra soothing effect.

EYE-GEL

Aloe's cooling properties make a great, quick, natural gel that tightens and tones the delicate skin around the eyes.
– DIRECTIONS: mash or blend the gel and pat gently around the eye area to refresh tired eyes. Rinse off or leave on as desired. If contact with the eyes occurs, rinse with warm water.

SHAVING GEL

Aloe also makes a brilliant natural shaving gel and is an effective alternative to the chemical-laden foams and creams found on shop shelves. Olive oil adds nourishing moisture and protection and again, you can also add two or three drops of essential oil to customise the fragrance.
– DIRECTIONS: blend the desired amount of gel with 1–2 tablespoons of olive oil. Apply to damp skin and shave as usual.

BEAUTY

1 kiwi fruit, at room
  temperature

3 tbsp ripe papaya, at room
  temperature

1 tbsp coconut oil (warmed to liquid)
1 tsp thick raw honey (see page 212)

PAPAYA & KIWI FACE MASK

RAW / VEGETARIAN

Makes 2
applications

With only plant-based ingredients, this is a nutrient-dense little treatment that will instantly awaken dull, tired skin. I avoid using manufactured face masks because they are usually overpriced, over-fragranced and full of chemicals and preservatives. But this nourishing and brightening recipe is packed with active fruit enzymes and two key natural beauty micronutrients: vitamin C, vital for collagen production and maintaining the skin's elasticity, and anti-inflammatory vitamin E, which helps protect the skin from free-radical damage and the associated ageing process. Coconut oil keeps skin soft and moisturised, while raw honey soothes and restores.

The leftover papaya makes a great addition to breakfast or a mid-treatment snack.

Start by scooping out the kiwi and mashing the flesh through a sieve into a bowl to make a smooth pulp, discarding the seeds and pith.

Mash the papaya flesh to a smooth paste. Combine in a bowl with the coconut oil, honey and kiwi and mix thoroughly by hand or with a blender. Chill in the fridge for 20 minutes to thicken. If you would like a thicker consistency, stir in a little more coconut oil and return to the fridge to set.

Apply to the face and neck and relax for 10–15 minutes. Rinse off with warm water.

Store any leftover face mask in an airtight container in the fridge for up to 2 days.

1 tsp beeswax
1 tbsp olive or coconut oil

½ tsp honey
4 drops of essential oil of your choice

BEESWAX & HONEY LIP BALM

VEGETARIAN

Makes 30g

Winter and chapped lips go hand in hand and this all-natural balm is a nourishing antidote. Most commercially manufactured lip balms contain harsh ingredients that do little to provide effective long-term moisture to this most delicate of areas. Petroleum jelly, a popular component, is the by-product of oil refining: it can sometimes contain residual carcinogens and blocks all our pores, preventing air and moisture from leaving or entering. Mineral oil, often used alongside petroleum jelly, has the same effect, and the result may seem like immediate relief from chapped lips but often leads to even dryer skin in the long term.

This alternative blend is 100% natural, and a little goes a long way. I also use it on excessively dry skin areas like my knees, elbows and nose if they need a little extra protection.

It lasts for up to 12 months and you can choose any fragrance you feel drawn to. I like citrus to uplift and remind me of summer.

Place the beeswax and oil in a small heatproof bowl and set over a pan of just simmering water, making sure the bottom of the bowl doesn't touch the water. You might want to use a dedicated beeswax bowl or jug to avoid putting any down the sink (see page 31).

Once the wax has melted and has mixed with the oil, wait until it is cool enough to comfortably leave your finger in (around 40°C) and quickly mix in the honey and essential oil.

Pour into a small jar or tin and leave to set for about 40 minutes at room temperature – or you can place it in the fridge to speed up the process. Store away from direct sunlight for up to 12 months.

BEAUTY

2 tsp oats
2 tsp ground almonds
½ tsp honey

1 tsp apple cider vinegar
2 drops of tea tree essential oil
¼ tsp bicarbonate of soda (optional)

ALMOND & TEA TREE FACE SCRUB

RAW / VEGETARIAN

Makes 1
application

This is a lovely, easy, everyday scrub that harnesses gentle natural ingredients to slough away dull skin and brighten the complexion. The oats contain soothing compounds called avenanthramides, which calm inflammation when applied to dry, sore or itchy skin. Here they work alongside a gentle team of complementary ingredients to exfoliate the face; they can also be used on their own as a soak to gently soothe the body: simply stuff a handful in a muslin bag or pair of clean old tights and place in the bath as an infusion.

The ground almonds provide gentle exfoliation, apple cider vinegar tones the complexion while antibacterial tea tree essential oil and soothing honey keep blemishes and breakouts at bay. The bicarbonate of soda is optional here – add it for extra exfoliation and deeper cleansing: it fizzes fantastically with the vinegar and creates a light, foamy mixture. Those with sensitive skin should stick to the original recipe.

You can make the scrub up as and when you need it, or make a larger batch (without the bicarbonate of soda) and store in an airtight jar. If the mixture dries out, just add a little water.

Mix all the ingredients together in a bowl and apply to damp skin. Gently exfoliate with your fingertips, avoiding the delicate eye area. Rinse thoroughly.

If you are making up a larger batch transfer to an airtight jar and store at room temperature and out of direct sunlight.

100ml castile soap
60ml honey
1 tbsp vitamin E oil

2 tbsp olive oil
20 drops of essential oil
(see below for suggestions)

EVERYDAY BODY WASH

RAW / VEGETARIAN

Makes 1 small
bottle or 10–15
applications

People are always surprised at how easy it is to make this body wash and love the ease with which you can customise the fragrance with essential oils. After using this, the shop-bought concoctions seem so fake and overpowering. It uses castile soap as its base, a traditional liquid soap that is a natural combination of plant-based oils (such as olive, hemp, coconut or almond), water and the alkali compound potassium hydroxide (which is there purely to facilitate the chemical reaction). You can buy various organic brands online or from the Fairtrade brand Dr Bronners. They have a wide range of options and also do fragranced blends to give you a head start.

The soothing honey and nourishing olive oil prevent dryness, and the aromatherapy options are endless. I use peppermint and tea tree to wake myself up in the morning and lavender and chamomile for calming evening baths.

The vitamin E oil acts as a natural preservative so make up a double batch and store it in your bathroom cabinet.

Mix all the ingredients together in a bottle with a tight-fitting lid. Store in the bottle and shake thoroughly before use in the bath or shower.

The body wash will keep for up to 3 months. In cooler climates, the oil may harden on top; simply soak the bottle in warm water before use.

DRY SKIN
BRUSHING

Dry skin brushing is an ancient natural beauty ritual. It promotes lymph circulation and helps us break down toxins stored around the body, as well as removing dead skin and bringing more oxygen to our cells to re-energise and regenerate. In tandem with regular exercise, it is a naturopathic exercise recommended for everyone, and is particularly helpful in breaking down cellulite.

The lymphatic system is the body's main immune network and in our sedentary lifestyles it can become stagnant and blocked. Waste products from reactions on our bodies' cells are gathered from tissues and eliminated through the lymph; many of its vessels lie just below the skin, so dry brushing is a quick and easy way to help stimulate this process, preventing congestion and the build-up of toxins. It also provides deep exfoliation on the surface of the skin and keeps it soft and smooth. As with the foot soak (see page 210) I like to use the time I spend brushing for a short meditation. The repetitive action and invigorating feeling it produces create a calming routine where I can drop the noises and demands of the mind and focus on the sensations of the body. This is especially welcome in the evening after long, busy days where a little re-energising and mental relaxation are called for.

All you need to dry brush is a natural hard bristle brush, or sisal mitt. The brush should have firm bristles and a long handle is helpful to reach your back unless you are wildly flexible. In my experience, the more you spend the better quality brush you will get and a well-made one can last you for years, so it's good to invest in the right one. In the morning, brush the whole body in long strokes on dry skin, from the feet upwards, always brushing towards the heart. Take care on sensitive areas at first; these will become accustomed to the bristles over time.

90g shea butter
90g coconut oil

90g beeswax
20 drops of essential oil (I use
   10 chamomile, 10 lavender)

SHEA BODY
LOTION BARS

VEGETARIAN

Makes 3 large
bars

These body bars are simple, pure and a little bit magical. Shea butter, a rich source of beneficial plant sterols and vitamin A, helps encourage the skin's natural repair and renewal process, improving the appearance of scars and lines, and soothing inflamed skin. Like jojoba, shea butter's oils also closely match those produced by our own sebaceous glands so are easily absorbed by the skin, making it a gentle natural moisturiser for sensitive or problem areas. Meanwhile, coconut oil's medium-chain fatty acids help soothe irritation and retain skin moisture. Its trio of capric, caprylic and lauric acids also provide antifungal and antibacterial protection, helping to keep rashes, infections and skin invaders at bay – particularly helpful for children with problematic or sensitive skin in need of some deep natural nourishment (see Beauty Heroes, page 206). Finally, rich honey-fragranced beeswax is a natural emulsifier and thickening agent, which binds the shea and coconut. It also contains vitamin A and works as a surfactant, locking in moisture while allowing the skin to breathe at the same time.

You can add any essential oil you like (see Aromatherapy, pages 238–41), and as all three main ingredients are used in equal parts you can easily scale the recipe up or down. I make mine in an old enamel muffin tin, but you could make a larger batch, pour into a loaf tin and slice into oblong bars.

Place the shea butter, coconut oil and beeswax in a heatproof bowl and set over a pan of just simmering water, making sure the bottom of the bowl doesn't touch the water. Melt the ingredients gently over a low-medium heat, stirring all the time until the mixture is melted.

Remove from the heat and continue to stir as you allow the mixture to cool a little before you add the essential oil. This is important as if the mixture is too hot, your oils will evaporate and go to waste. I try and leave it until just before it starts to thicken. Stir in the essentials oils and pour into a muffin tin. Leave to set at room temperature for 3–4 hours (you can also place them in the fridge to speed up the setting process).

Once the bars are hard, remove from the tin and store in greaseproof paper at room temperature and away from direct sunlight. Apply to clean, dry skin after bathing or showering, as an all-over body treat or just to particularly dry areas. The warmer your skin, the softer the bar will become; if it is cool and hard, warm it between your hands before use.

The bars will keep for up to 6 months.

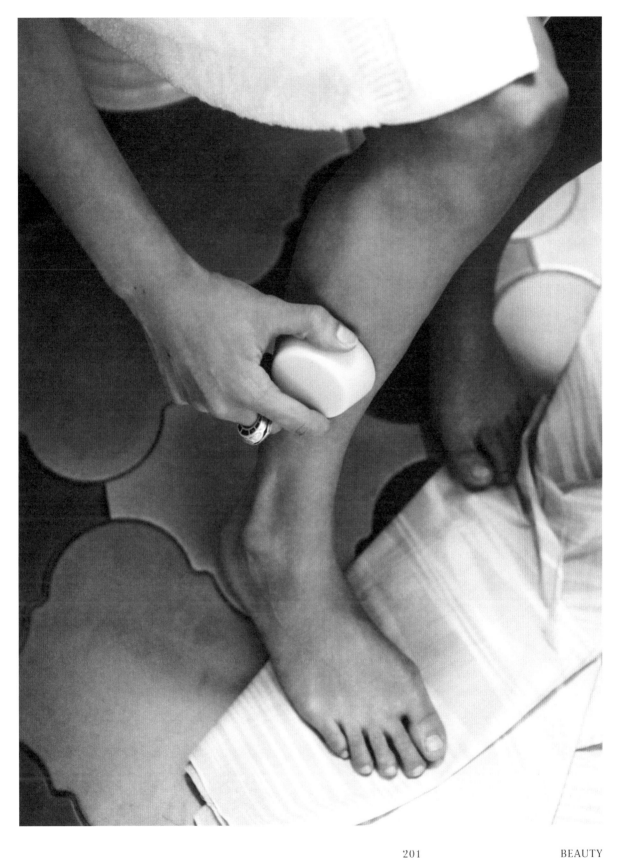

BEAUTY

250ml water
2 tbsp apple cider vinegar

5 drops of tea tree or chamomile
    essential oil

APPLE CIDER HAIR RINSE

RAW / VEGAN

Makes 1
application

Among its many nutritional benefits (helping to optimise the stomach pH, balance blood sugar and support the lymphatic system), apple cider vinegar is also a powerful natural beauty hero. It is toning when used in dilution on the skin, yet softening on the hair, and as versatile as it is nourishing.

This simple rinse leaves your locks feeling shiny and renewed: the acetic acid in the vinegar gently breaks down residue from regular shampooing and conditioning, leaving your scalp and hair soft and clean. (Diluted with a little more water and applied to a cotton pad, this recipe also doubles up as a natural facial toner.) Always choose vinegar that is raw, unpasteurised and undiluted for the best results.

The essential oils are a great way to customise the recipe according to your preference, but not vital. I choose chamomile for extra shine, and tea tree if my scalp is feeling a little on the oily side.

Mix all the ingredients in a jug or cup. After shampooing, apply the rinse to the scalp and hair and leave on for 10 minutes. Rinse thoroughly and follow with conditioner if needed.

You can make small batches as you need it, or multiply the quantities for busy family bathrooms. It will keep in an airtight container for up to 12 months, away from direct sunlight.

2 tbsp rosehip oil
1 tbsp jojoba oil

10 drops of essential oil – try orange
and tea tree, or rose and geranium

1 tsp vitamin E oil

HERBAL NIGHT OIL

RAW / VEGAN

Makes 60ml

I love this simple, nourishing night oil just before bed, especially in the colder months. The rich red rosehip is a natural source of collagen-stimulating vitamin C and a compound called transretinoic acid, brilliant for soothing inflamed skin (whether down to dryness, a rash or spots), healing scars and protecting against free-radical damage to the skin. I often use it to help heal mild burn scars (every cook's bête noire) as it encourages the healing process without any harsh chemicals or additives.

The vitamin E oil acts a natural preservative (and can be used as such in most natural beauty recipes). It also provides a little further anti-inflammatory support, while the structure of the lighter jojoba closely matches our own skin's natural sebum, keeping our skin's oil production in balance and allowing it to breathe while receiving maximum nourishment.

If you make this in small batches, you can choose your essential oils according to preference. Citrus is especially uplifting in the summer months, while rose and geranium are a calming floral combination that I use throughout autumn and winter. You can find rosehip and jojoba oils at many high street retailers; always choose cold-pressed and organic.

Combine all the ingredients in a dark glass bottle.

Shake well before massaging a small amount onto the face and neck before bed. Store in a cool, dark place out of direct sunlight for up to 6 months.

NATURAL BEAUTY HERO: COCONUT OIL

Coconut oil is a true naturopathic hero, not only in the kitchen but the bathroom too. As well as providing rich plant-based moisturisation, it also has anti-inflammatory and antibacterial properties and can be used for a whole host of natural beauty purposes. It is a robust, stable oil, easy to produce sustainably and organically, and in many cases far more cost effective than its factory-produced counterparts.

The main compound found in coconut oil is lauric acid. This fatty acid is the most similar in structure to human mother's milk, and supports the body's metabolic processes as well as providing antimicrobial and antifungal protection. It is converted by the body into a compound called monolaurin, which can help support immunity – both when consumed and applied to the skin – by inhibiting the growth of common viruses and invaders. It also contains capric acid and caprylic acid, which further protect against fungi and microbes: all-in-all a powerful friend that gently protects and softens our bodies' largest organ, the skin.

If you do not like the nutty scent, you can opt for the flavourless version, but make sure it has been distilled through steaming and not bleaching or high temperature processing.

MOISTURISER

High in fatty acids, coconut oil makes a brilliant all-over moisturiser. While most conventional manufactured body creams contain water, which gives the sensation of moisture but dries on the skin relatively quickly after being applied, oils like coconut provide deeper nourishment and avoid the many chemical compounds used to make modern lotions, creams and butters. It is also absorbed relatively quickly and a little goes a long way.

As a facial moisturiser, its antibacterial properties can help fight breakouts; those with oily skin can benefit by using it sparingly and gently building up to a regular routine.
– DIRECTIONS: apply a thin layer all over the body or on the desired area after bathing or showering. Used with a soft cotton pad or warm muslin cloth, it is also great for removing make-up.

HAIR TREATMENT

Coconut oil is a brilliant one-ingredient hair treatment and gives shine and vitality to dry locks. I always take a pot on holiday and it takes care of all my beauty needs, whatever the sun, sand and sea might throw at me. While many oils simply coat the hair and are then rinsed out, coconut oil's unique structure means it can penetrate the hair shaft and provide deep nourishment from within.
– DIRECTIONS: comb through dry hair and leave on for 20–30 minutes before washing it as usual with warm water.

PULLING

Pulling with coconut oil is an ancient method of mouth hygiene and an attractive natural complement to modern toothpastes to help fight gum disease, bad breath, inflammation and cavities. Kept in the mouth for 15 minutes, the oil suffocates bacteria and helps remove toxins and break down plaque. It also has a natural tooth-whitening effect and is a much safer, less corrosive alternative to harsh commercial whiteners.
– DIRECTIONS: before brushing your teeth, take a spoonful of coconut oil at room temperature and swish it around your mouth for 15 minutes

(or as long as you can; it takes time to build up the habit). Try making a smoothie or preparing breakfast to keep you busy during the process. This is most effective when done in the morning as our bodies perform their major detoxification during the night. When you are finished, dispose of the oil in the bin and brush your teeth as usual. Use as a natural alternative to mouthwash, daily if you wish but once a week is fine too.

a large bowl or tub of warm water
   (at bath temperature)
1 tbsp Epsom salts

10 drops of essential oil
1 tsp bicarbonate of soda (optional)

BACK TO LIFE FOOT SOAK

RAW / *VEGAN*

Makes 1 soak

Anyone who works on their feet all day will know the joy of a good restorative foot soak (and the magic of Birkenstocks), and this magnesium-rich one has been known to rejuvenate even the weariest toes. They may seem a little old school, but foot soaks are a quick, easy and deeply relaxing way to reinvigorate the body and the senses, and with some 250,000 sweat glands on the soles of our feet, a short dip in nourishing salts can have miraculous effects. Our feet bear so much weight and activity each day; I find that if we relax and restore them, the rest of the body happily follows suit.

Epsom salts (magnesium sulphate crystals) are a favourite naturopathic tool, absorbed transdermally (through the skin) via a bath or soak. The boost of magnesium – a mineral we need plenty of for optimal cell function and in which we can often become deficient – promotes muscle relaxation and deep sleep; the sulphate supports the body's detoxification and breakdown of chemicals and environmental toxins, and the salts support the body's circulation and soften skin. When you need to rejuvenate tired muscles, clear noisy thoughts and can't sink back into a long bath, a quick foot soak is a lovely alternative.

I like to use a combination of peppermint and tea tree essential oils for ultimate refreshment; you can also add some bicarbonate of soda for extra skin softening.

Mix all the ingredients together in a large tub or bowl and swirl to dissolve the salts.

Sit comfortably and soak the feet for 15–20 minutes. Use this time to quieten the mind and relax into the body. Reconnect to the breath and experience the sensations around you: focus your attention on the warm water surrounding your feet and the soothing aromas of the essential oils, quietly turning within.

When you are finished, dry your feet, pour away the soak and be mindful of any differences you feel both physically and emotionally.

NATURAL BEAUTY HERO: HONEY

Honey is one of the oldest and most healing beauty aids known to man. The ancient Egyptians used it as a natural skin softener and Cleopatra famously soaked regularly in milk and honey baths – not for nothing: it is a deeply nourishing and versatile topical ingredient, offering benefits for all skin types. To be more specific, honey is what is known as a natural humectant, which means it traps moisture on the skin to prevent dryness. It also contains a wealth of minerals including magnesium, zinc, sodium, potassium, iron and calcium. It has a high antioxidant content, including vitamin C, chrysin, pinobanksin and catalase, which help scavenge free radicals and prevent oxidative damage to the skin. Last, but not least, it has antibacterial properties.

The widespread availability and gentleness of honey make it a brilliant natural beauty staple, suitable for children and those with sensitive skin. For optimal benefits, it is important to use raw honey that has not been altered through processing or heat.

ANTIBACTERIAL PROTECTION

Honey's high viscosity and antibacterial action make it an effective natural treatment for minor wounds, burns and irritated skin. Like aloe vera (see Beauty Hero, page 190), it forms a protective and moist barrier on the skin which promotes healing; combined with a high sugar content, acidic composition and the production of hydrogen peroxide, it helps fight off infections and appears to stimulate the body's immune cells. For wounds it is important to use Manuka honey: it is sterilised, lab-tested for medicinal purposes and given a UMF (Unique Manuka Factor): the higher the number, the greater the antibacterial activity (see page 26).
– TO TREAT MILD WOUNDS: clean the wound, burn or irritated area, apply a thin layer of honey to a sterile dressing and leave on for as long as possible. Re-apply twice a day as needed. If wounds are infected or resistant to healing, you should seek medical advice immediately.

FACE MASK

A natural honey face mask harnesses all the above benefits and can leave irritated or acne-prone skin smoother, softer and less prone to breakouts. It is gentle enough to be used for all skin types, and will not interfere with acne medication. You can also mix it with a teaspoon of aloe vera, for extra moisture, or blended apple (the apple contains malic acid, which promotes gentle natural exfoliation).
–DIRECTIONS: wash your face and gently pat it dry. Apply a thin layer of honey to the desired area with clean hands, leave on for 15–20 minutes and rinse thoroughly. Repeat up to three times a week as desired.

HAIR MASK

When mixed with a carrier such as water or apple cider vinegar, honey's humectant action provides extra moisturisation for dry hair, and a healthy natural shine; very damaged or unruly locks can be further tamed with a little added olive oil. The below guidelines will get you started but the ratio of ingredients depends on the thickness and length of your hair: play around and see what works best for you, each head is different.
– DIRECTIONS: in a bowl, mix around 3 tablespoons of honey with 3–4 tablespoons of apple cider vinegar or warm water to form a thin mask that will lightly cover your head. Comb through shampooed hair, leave on for 15–20 minutes, rinse thoroughly and condition as normal. If you are using

olive oil, mix one part oil with two parts honey, and add a little warm water to thin it out if necessary. Apply in the same way as the basic mask and shampoo twice before conditioning. Use once a week or as necessary.

SCRUB

In Russian-style banyas (saunas) honey is often mixed with coffee and used as an invigorating, cellulite-busting scrub. I like to do this with my leftover grounds as it gives them a new lease of life and is a quick, easy and cost-effective natural beauty treatment. Simply rinse your used coffee, store in a bowl in the fridge and mix with a little runny honey before your shower to form a thick but malleable paste. How much honey you use depends on your coffee and personal preference, but the mixture should be relatively fluid; sometimes you may like to use less for a really strong and deep exfoliation, or more for a thinner, gentler consistency. You can add a little water if your honey is on the thicker side. Apply the scrub immediately to damp skin, exfoliate and rinse thoroughly.

35ml water
50ml orange flower water
5ml jojoba oil

10 drops of essential oil – bergamot,
lemon or grapefruit go well

ORANGE FLOWER SKIN & HAIR SPRITZ

RAW / VEGAN

Makes 100ml

Orange flower water is the by-product of the distillation of orange flower blossom for essential oil, and while it is often used in Middle Eastern cooking, it also makes an exotic and effective natural beauty ally. It has a delicious, uplifting fragrance, is mildly astringent (toning and tightening the skin) but gentle enough for sensitive skin, and widely available in food shops, although you should always opt for organic.

Mixed here with a small amount of jojoba and essential oils, it makes a light everyday pick-me-up spray for skin and hair in need of some refreshment, and the uplifting citrus aromas help rejuvenate the senses. I like to keep a bottle at home and one in my bag for travels and adventures: whether navigating hot humid climes or rush hour on the London Underground, a quick spray diffuses daily grit and grime in an instant.

You can also make this with rosewater; its deeper scent is particularly uplifting in the winter months and goes well with calming lavender or chamomile essential oils.

Mix the water and orange flower water in a 100ml glass spray bottle, and then add the jojoba and essential oil(s). Shake well before you spritz on to skin or hair.

Keeps for up to 6 months stored away from direct sunlight.

Part 3

MINDFUL LIVING

Just like our bodies, our spirits need nourishing too, and in my experience living more mindfully is as important to our wellbeing as a balanced diet and natural skincare. In fact, meditation and mindful eating are the fundamental actions from which all wellness springs. There was a time when I would have denied their relevance to my far-too-busy life, racing through my days with the noise of my thoughts bursting in my head, but the sacred space I have learned to cultivate within is the most enriching part of my whole journey, and one I feel drawn to share within the framework of modern life.

Gratitude, intention, awareness and presence are such fleeting concepts in our frantic twenty-first-century existence, but learning to nurture them in all that we do is vital if we are to live as balanced, harmonious beings that reach our full vitality and potential. The tools and rituals in this chapter are those that have kept me rooted in the here and now, every day, whether hawking gyoza in the van or writing at home on my own; through them I am reminded that spirituality and a connection to the sacred around us doesn't have to be achieved on far-flung retreats or intensive workshops. It is within us all, and just needs awakening. From everyday mindfulness to simple aromatherapy blends and working with crystals, there are many wonderful ways to tread the path and once you begin it just keeps on expanding.

5 TOOLS FOR EVERYDAY MINDFULNESS

Being present in everyday life is not easy for us twenty-first-century humans. We may occasionally find the time to quiet the mind but there comes a point in every person's week when the noise of the to-do list takes over and defeats even the most accomplished modern buddha. Practising these five simple tools is a powerful way to tap into our inner skies, interrupt unhelpful thought patterns and meet with the present moment in all its fullness.

DAILY MEDITATION

Meditation is a basic need in order to find balance in our overcomplicated, technology-fuelled lives. It is something that will give a rich foundation to everything we do. Simply sitting with the self and drawing the senses inward for 15 minutes a day is such a powerful habit to cultivate, and if you really struggle to begin with start with just 5 minutes. Find somewhere quiet and just be with your breath; try to watch any feelings and ideas as they pass through your mind, as though from a distance and without attaching to them – all that is required is the willingness to look inside. By not judging, but observing our thoughts like clouds in the sky, we come to know ourselves with a new depth and acceptance.

SETTING AN INTENTION

Sometimes the word 'intention' sends us into a spiral of panic. We trip out because we do not know what we want, what we would like, how we think we should be, what our heart is telling us. But the power of intentions is so strong even if they're very small and simple. In fact, for me, that is exactly what they must be. Creating a basic focus for the day cuts through all the noise and calls of duty; it is a gift to yourself that you can fall back on when things shift and change and you lose your ground. Today I will listen; today I will be present for whomever or whatever is in front of me; today I feel like the sky is falling down but I will invite only positive thoughts…

Setting a daily intention and giving it up to your altar (see page 231) is a gentle way to step back and look at where you are in your life. Ask yourself what you need and then build your day around it, brick by brick. Become your own compass.

LISTEN TO THE WISDOM OF THE BODY

The body holds the strongest wisdom yet is so often the first thing to be ignored when the going gets rough and the days are filled with coffee and running and doing and surviving. This is how we become unstuck and physical and emotional imbalance sets in.

Take time each day to pause and ask your body what it wants. We were built to eat slowly and with very little choice; with so much to choose from now and so little time for mealtimes, we end up grabbing the nearest thing and devouring it on the move, even if it isn't what we truly need. Learning to hear the body's signals is an amazing tool to keep us connected and healthy every day, every time we are about to put something in our mouths. Ask your body what it really wants, and listen properly when it tells you to slow down.

RESPECT YOUR BOUNDARIES

Knowing our boundaries begets a self-respect and honesty that bring a little more clarity into each day. So many interactions in daily life require something of us and if you are a 'yes' person you will inevitably smile and say 'sure thing' to most demands. I have done this by default for years, and it can drain our energy and presence fast. It's not easy to rewire the response, but with a little awareness it can turn into something more honest. Respecting your inner voice enough to say no, express discomfort or just not get involved is an amazing tool in life and one that's easy to practise every day, whatever the situation.

With a daily awareness of this, when we do say yes, it is from a place of truth and presence. Explore your boundaries tomorrow and see how you feel expressing them.

DAILY GRATITUDE

At the end of the daily scramble there is always something to be grateful for, but sometimes the troubles that came alongside can eclipse the rest of the landscape. Nothing is more healing than remembering what we have and what we are thankful for: the fundamentals of life that give us back our perspective.

Acknowledging our daily gratitudes, no matter how small, creates a positive space to come back to when life gets challenging and we are losing ground. How we perceive our lives dictates the journey of our days, and remembering what we have is just as easy as forgetting it. In times when life is hardest, expressing what you're grateful for each day is a little window into a world we thought we left behind; a simple reminder of what makes you smile.

OJOS
DE DIOS

In Mexican Huichol culture, the Ojo de Dios (or God's eye) is a fortuitous symbol and meditative craft, invoking the all-seeing knowledge of the divine and asking for protection and blessings at home or on the road. It is traditionally woven with brightly coloured yarn around two perpendicular sticks, whose four points represent the elements: earth, water, wind and fire; while the omniscient eye created by the woven yarn keeps watch. They are great talismans to make and a really fun way to invite some goodness into your life. We made them at a wellness event I organised one winter for over 80 Londoners and the peace and focus around the table was a wonderful thing to behold. Kids adore them too and the simple process leaves them plenty of room to focus and be present. I like to gather a couple of sticks from nature when I go to the countryside, but anything wooden and equal in length will work.

HOW TO MAKE
AN OJO DE DIOS

You will need two sticks of equal length and yarn in at least two different colours. Place the sticks together at a perpendicular angle to make a cross and secure them with a knot of yarn. Start to weave the first colour of yarn around the centre of the cross in a diamond formation, looping it around round each stick as you pass it. Carry on until you have made a small diamond and then change colours. Keep going, changing the yarn colours as you go, until you are happy with the design. Secure the end with a knot and place it above your doorway or hang from it a tree or window. The more, the merrier.

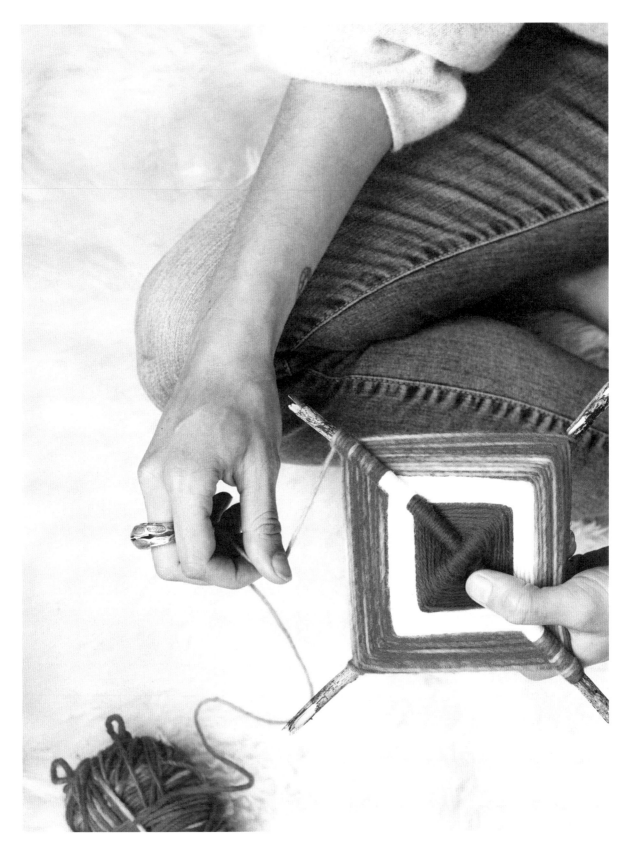

MINDFUL LIVING

MINDFUL EATING

Mindful eating is one of the basic precepts of naturopathic nutrition and something that doesn't come easily in the busy modern age. Our immunity, nutrient absorption and overall vitality all begin with the digestive system. When we race around eating our lunch while running down the street or checking our phones, the gut is not best prepared to absorb the nutrients and so comes under sudden and unexpected strain. This can lead to all sorts of imbalance and disease so eating with awareness, gratitude and presence encourages a return to an optimal state where we are ready to receive nutrients and energy.

TRY TO PREPARE AT LEAST ONE MEAL A DAY

Just a few decades ago we spent a good number of hours in the kitchen each day preparing our food, yet now we are in the minority if we dedicate more than a few minutes a day. The act of cooking is so important with regard to our digestive processes: it stimulates the stomach to release peptic acids and prepare for digestion, and while our insides have hardly changed over all these years, our cooking habits have – often with negative effects on our health and vitamin and mineral status. A return to wholefood preparation is as beneficial to our gut as it is to society, and it can start with something as simple as a smoothie, some nut milk or a bowl of porridge for breakfast (see pages 38, 48, 52, 53, 57 or 164).

CULTIVATE GRATITUDE

One of the tenets of the macrobiotic diet is acknowledging gratitude for the food in front of you, whether you have cooked it or not, and practising this is a more profound way to connect to your body and what you put in it. Build a habit of taking a moment at mealtimes – no matter how brief or imperceptible to others – to quietly close your eyes and give thanks for the food before you. By cultivating an awareness of where our food comes from and the goodness it provides us, we forge a dynamic relationship with what we put into our bodies and foster an attitude of responsibility for it.

EAT WITH AWARENESS

Many of those who seek nutritional help see dramatic benefits when they start to approach their meals with more presence and focus. Leaving technology aside during mealtimes, placing your knife and fork down between each mouthful and chewing thoroughly are three simple things we can do to help our body make the most of the fuel we are giving it. A large proportion of digestion begins in the mouth, and yet rarely do we chew our food nearly as much as we should. With proper breakdown in the mouth, by the time our sustenance reaches the stomach it is in the best state possible for maximum nutrient breakdown and absorption.

It is also helpful to use one meal a week (or even a day) as a meditation: an opportunity to practise noticing how you feel as you eat your food, how your body reacts to it, and what physical effects occur after. Often through this focused attention we realise that what we thought we craved and needed is not in fact giving us the most vitality, or is even slowing us down, straining our digestive systems or contributing to inflammation. A food diary, where you note everything you eat and how you feel after, is another very useful way to monitor this and can reveal unseen links between food groups and unwelcome symptoms.

COMMUNITY

From as global as how you choose your food and clothes to as local as the family and friends you surround yourself with, tapping into a real-life community seems to me to be so important if we are to reach our full potential together. The internet and social media unite us in many ways, but they also allow us to stay physically isolated while maintaining social contacts, giving us a feeling of connection as face-to-face encounters fade increasingly into the background. Tapping into a genuine community and spending a few hours (even weeks, months) physically surrounded by like-minded humans – our brothers and sisters on this planet we inhabit – gives us vital support, inspiration, knowledge and friendship with which to navigate our lives. The authenticity and vulnerability that come with connecting with one another face to face are at the essence of what makes us human; sharing life together in all its pain and glory is the key to growth, expansion and peace as individuals and as a collective. After all… no man (or woman) is an island.

CONSUMER COMMUNITY

Whether you choose to buy local, organic, Fairtrade, sustainable, ethical or recycled, joining a consumer community in your everyday food, fashion and lifestyle choices opens the door to shared values and a common vision for humanity – wherever you live. Through supporting these global movements, we transcend our own social groups and local identities to connect with all those who value the same ideals as us. These conscious choices bring some love and intention into our everyday shopping and it can be so refreshing to discover, and be reminded, that even when we buy some tea, spinach or a new sweater, we can be part of a movement that is much greater than ourselves.

LOCAL COMMUNITIES

It doesn't have to be global: anywhere where there is local, organic food or yoga or meditation – anything that makes you tick – there is a conscious community to tap into and like-minded humans to get to know. Go to your local farmers' market and have a chat to the suppliers; find a local pottery, supper club, evening course or group and connect with the people you meet there. Putting down these roots based on choices rather than old social patterns is the first step to exploring a new creative or spiritual direction. The street-food community was such a vibrant source of inspiration and one of the main reasons why Ben and I felt so compelled to set up Rainbo; similarly, in my nutrition studies, I have connected with so many fascinating kindred spirits as we pursue the common goal of wellness. Whatever your passion, find your kin there, and support each other on the journey.

FEMALE COMMUNITY

As a woman navigating modern life and all its various demands, it can be so easy to feel isolated, both physically and emotionally, from our fellow female tribe. Careers, technology and ever-shifting roles mean we often develop a system of living where time spent together as women, and nothing more, is rare or even non-existent. Connecting honestly with my sisters from all walks of life, both in the flesh and via social media, has been an invaluable support as I enter my thirties and is, I believe, a very strong medicine for the modern female psyche. We used to live together in communities and pass through life's stages alongside one another; in many areas of modern culture this tribal nature has been lost and we are losing access to the healing that can arise when we navigate our rites of passage together. That is not to say that there is no space for men: there is plenty, and they are very good at gathering together; but some things only your own gender can understand and, in my own experience, I feel stronger as a woman and as a human when I dedicate time to open, honest sharing with my female friends. There are many women's circles growing in cities and communities across the world: find one and see where it takes you… it might be somewhere beautiful.

SHARING

Sharing is healing: almost any time we put down our barriers and are open about how we are feeling, we are strengthened by the process.

And yet in the age we live in, it can be a real challenge to find the space and time in which to do it. Life moves so quickly: lunches with a friend last an hour if we are lucky; meanwhile social media feeds show us glimpses into picture-perfect lives we wish we could have, and the scope for authentic expression of life's ups and downs can seem a little limited. True vulnerability, and the space in which to explore it, is increasingly rare and yet so important to our overall wellness.

The premise of sharing is that you are able to open your heart and express how you are feeling without being met with any judgment, advice or response. Simply to say 'I feel sad, overwhelmed, joyous, lucky, confused, exhausted, inadequate, conflicted or just a little bit nothing right now' – and be heard – is a powerful means of recognising what is going on for us at a certain moment, and acknowledging it. Then it can pass. It is not the job of the other to interpret, console or react: they are simply holding space.

The other great value in sharing is that you are placed in a position in which you can really hear what others are going through and this can be enormously humbling and grounding. Tuning into the joys, hopes and fears of others takes the focus away from the self, reminding us that we all share the same struggles and are not that different after all; perhaps we can find an opportunity there to support someone else in a way we had never thought of before.

SHARING WITH A PARTNER

In relationships, speaking in turn can be a really helpful tool when communication isn't flowing easily. Taking away the potential for reaction, blame or judgment, sharing allows each partner to say what's on their mind and track their feelings freely.

It can be nice to do this first thing in the morning or last thing before bed, after a little meditation, as a means of checking in. Create a comfortable space sitting opposite one another. Perhaps you want to cleanse the air with a little palo santo (see page 228), or light a candle or some incense to create a sense of intention. Then meet your partner with your eyes, and take it in turns to say how you are feeling emotionally (but also physically if it is affecting you in your body) with no interruption or input from the other. Four or five minutes is usually a good time for each. Then thank your partner for their honesty and their listening.

Often we find that if our beloved says something hurtful or to which we feel the urgent need to react, by the time the session has passed, the impulse has gone and we are able to respond, instead of react, in a calm and measured way.

SHARING WITH FRIENDS

It is also wonderful to get together with some friends – whether a few or a big gathering – and create a space where you can share. I like to think of it as a conscious dinner party, one which you leave feeling strengthened and inspired (instead of drunk and a little blurry). If you feel a little daunted by talking openly about yourself, it is easier to start with just one or two friends. Prepare some food and make a lovely table – you might also have a potluck supper where you each bring a culinary creation. Then go round the table in a circle and simply say where you are at and how you feel. It's a nice way to open up together and often we touch on common themes that we do not habitually discuss.

Avoiding alcohol is a good idea so that things keep their focus and authenticity. If you're with friends or a group you trust, you'd be amazed how easily we open up and how quickly our social fears and taboos fly out the window: everyone has something to teach you.

CLEANSING YOUR SPACE

Modern life throws an ever-increasing array of unwanted toxins and stresses our way and cultivating the habit of cleansing our space, as well as our bodies, is an empowering step towards a more mindful way of living. Wi-Fi, mobile phones, environmental pollution and general city living at close quarters can often make it difficult for us to achieve a sense of calm and openness, but with a few simple rituals you can create a sacred space where meditation comes more easily and which you can call your own, wherever you live.

SMUDGING WITH SAGE

This aromatic herb has long been revered by many cultures for its cleansing and clarifying properties, and a bundle of dried leaves (known as a smudge stick) is never far away in our home. Lighting it and clearing any space from old beliefs, negative energy or just stagnant air with its aroma, or smudging, is a powerful means of resetting, both emotionally and physically. Take a few moments beforehand to connect to your intention, then light the sage over a candle and blow it out after a minute or so, letting the dried leaves glow and smolder. Waft it around the room and fill every nook and corner with its aromatic smoke; now is a good time to bid farewell to the old and welcome in the new, whatever that may be. To smudge yourself or someone else, move the sage around the whole body, front and back, and visualise any negative emotions and energy evaporating with the smoke – you can also use a large feather to fan it. This can be a powerful way to emotionally reset and is a lovely ritual to do with a friend or partner.

PALO SANTO

The sweet scent of palo santo – or holy wood – is an integral part of many shamanic ceremonies and the sacred tree is becoming increasingly present in our own cultures as we embark on deepening journeys of self-discovery. This distinctive, aromatic wood is native to South America and belongs to the same family as frankincense and myrrh. Like sage, it is burned and used to cleanse the space, and it possesses antibacterial properties and a fragrant aroma. Lighting a stick before meditation is both invigorating and purifying; building the daily ritual of smudging the room with it to cleanse the space upon waking is another gentle way to cultivate intention and welcome each new day in all its glory.

You can also use it alongside the stronger scent of sage for more poignant moments, when a greater sense of purification is called for, or to cleanse objects and items that may hold negative connotations or leftover negativity. Smudging in this way is a symbolic fresh start, a means of clearing stagnant energy and protecting your own living space from surrounding negativity or disharmony.

SINGING BOWLS

I first heard crystal singing bowls in the forest in Costa Rica and their soothing harmony has intrigued me ever since. I am not musical at all but my beloved quartz bowl is one of my most prized meditation tools and whenever I play it, something shifts for me and for those in the room. Sound healers, therapists and meditators all over are increasingly drawn to singing bowls for their ability to realign the chakras and rid the body of stagnant energy: the harmonic sounds are a beautiful way to open your daily meditation and create a sense of transition into a sacred space. They are wonderfully intuitive to use and you do not need to 'learn' to play one: simply circling the outer rim with the wand produces a soft harmonic vibration. Faster movements create a stronger sound, while a gentle tap two thirds of the way up gives a gentle chime. You can get many different sizes of bowl (corresponding to different notes and their chakras) in a variety of crystals. Feel your way around the sounds and find out which speeds and techniques feel most comfortable for you: just as the 'ohm' unites us all in one voice, the bowls set a unique resonance and frequency in which to gently turn inwards.

MINDFUL LIVING

MAKING
AN ALTAR

An expressive space for memories, intention and purpose, an altar is a lovely opportunity to focus our attention on what we are grateful for, what we want to manifest, and give definition to our sources of inspiration. With life moving as fast as it does, it can be all too easy to lose sight of our hopes, dreams, passions and all the love and beauty that surrounds us. Remembering and meditating on this within the framework of an altar, we remember what is important to us and invite ourselves to turn inwards and explore our inner skies with clear intentions. Making your own devotional altar in the home is a wonderful creative process: it is like a living diary of where we have been and what we have experienced, a physical reflection of what matters to us the most and where we are at in our lives and relationships.

HOW TO MAKE AN ALTAR

In my own altar at home I like to place trinkets and talismans from travels and happy times in my past – a constant reminder of what I have to be grateful for. Here are some ideas to create your own altar.

· A colourful fabric covering or clean, earthy texture such as wood or ceramic makes a good setting, linking to cultures and traditions that we resonate with, or the earth itself. Flowers or a plant remind us of our synergy with nature and bring an other-worldly beauty and energy.

· Incense and candles fill the room with warmth and comfort and create a sense of sacred space in which to meditate.

· If you feel drawn to crystals they are a beautiful addition to an altar (for more on crystals see pages 234–5).

· If there is a particular theme or concern in your life that you need help with, that you've thought and thought about until your mind is crazy and it's now down to your heart to figure out, find a way to bring it in to the altar. Express it on paper or find a physical object that represents it and then make friends with it: get to know it in your heart and body. Often it is from this deeper space that we find a little more resolution and clarity and the helicopter mind can quieten down and return to what it needs to focus on.

· I also have a little pouch in which I take my favourite little altar objects when I travel. It started with a few tiny crystals for companionship and keeps growing: it helps create a devotional space in which to stay centered wherever I am, a little reminder of mindfulness and inspiration.

Just like our gardens and our homes, our spirits need some nurturing too: take some time today to make yourself an altar and create a space of love and devotion in which to explore yours. It is one of the loveliest projects to embark upon, and constantly evolves as you do.

CRYSTALS

Crystals make a beautiful meditation aid, and for centuries their varying formations have been attributed specific healing potential. Each crystal formed in the earth has its own unique lattice structure, which dictates how electromagnetic energies move through it. Quartz, for example, has a very stable structure and is used as an electromagnetic regulator in clocks, and to receive signals in radios. Those who work with crystals for healing believe that other energies that we cannot see can also be transmuted through them, and use various stones to amplify, absorb or redirect the flow of a certain force within and around us. Learning to connect with crystals in this way can be a rewarding and empowering journey; this is particularly true in the digital age where Wi-Fi and unseen frequencies and radio waves surround us from dawn till dusk.

For some the connection to a certain stone can be almost instantaneous, and its potential felt physically upon first contact; for others, it can take a while. In my experience, the very act of tuning in and assessing which stone feels exciting to us, and what we would like to rebalance with it, is another way to help us scan our inner landscape and naturally re-establish inner harmony.

A good place to start is to gradually collect the ones that draw your eye and live with them around your space. I have a trusty collection, formed over the years from travels and gifts, that I keep around me at home and on the move. Simply placing them by my bed, yoga mat or meditation chair, I call to mind their individual properties and take stock of how I am feeling, what might need clearing in the air and what qualities I would like to invite into my waking or sleeping.

Other times I might choose to hold a certain stone during a meditation and simply notice how I feel in doing so; one day it might be amethyst to help counter unhelpful excesses; another it may be labradorite to help reconnect to my true purpose. In times of stress or sadness it can also be helpful to direct that excess energy to the stone itself and envisage the flow of tension out of the body and mind; visualisation can be such a powerful tool.

I also keep a few favourite crystals on my altar (see page 231), to absorb my daily intentions and act as a reminder of my journey on this path to wellness.

AMETHYST

Amethyst is a form of quartz combined with manganese, and additional iron creates its beautiful purple hue. It has been used throughout history to protect from overindulgence and intoxication, keeping us grounded in states of higher consciousness and pursuit of passion. Its high frequency is said to allow us to remain centred while exploring the spiritual realm and developing our intuition, creativity and expression.

LABRADORITE

Labradorite is held as a particularly useful crystal in today's digital world, known for calming busy minds and strengthening our powers of intuition – often underdeveloped in a world of so much choice. With its iridescent rainbow sheen, it is used to connect with the unseen spiritual realm where self-awareness and inner guidance can be cultivated. It is a stone of self-discovery and a welcome friend when we feel we have lost our way on the spiritual path.

OBSIDIAN

Obsidian is recognised as one of the most protective crystals, and is believed to be able to shield us from negative energy. This can be particularly helpful in crowded situations when we feel imposed upon by others, as well as in spiritual journeying. Mirroring the intensity of its dark black volcanic gleam, it can bring negative emotions to the surface, surfacing past traumas and forcing us to confront what must be examined. In this capacity, it is seen as a very powerful tool on the road to self-discovery, showing us truth in all its guises. The result is greater harmony, balance and awareness of our true nature.

OPAL

Harnessing the full beauty of the rainbow, opal's magical luminescence is difficult to ignore. It is often used to help break through emotional darkness, bringing light and illumination to all aspects of our aura and self. Opal is often referred to as the karmic stone, reflecting what we put out, and this can be a useful focus in self-reflection as we turn our attention to our behaviour towards others.

QUARTZ

Known as the universal crystal, clear quartz makes a wonderful altar centerpiece or travelling companion. It is thought of as a balancing stone, absorbing surrounding energy and so neutralising and protecting us from modern interrupters such as Wi-Fi, electromagnetic waves and environmental pollution. Within the same capacity it is thought to strengthen and balance the chakras and activate our own inner energy; this stabilising capacity makes it an ideal companion for meditation and healing.

BAREFOOT
EARTHING

Barefoot walking, or earthing, is one of the simplest ways to instantly ground ourselves. I find this particularly beneficial in the city, where we can so easily become disconnected from our natural environment. Kicking our shoes off for a walk in the park is an instantaneous way to press 'reset' and reconnect with nature when we are caught up in everyday stresses. It also gets us out in the sunshine for a good and often-needed dose of vitamin D.

When we touch the ground with the soles of our feet, exposing all their thousands of specialised pores, we are able to absorb the earth's electrons. These are thought to function as antioxidants within the body, eliminating free radicals and reducing the inflammation they can cause, and also help to balance the autonomic nervous system, which controls our stress response mechanisms. We spend so much more time in the sympathetic (or 'fight or flight') state than we used to and the negative effects on our health are easily recognisable as widespread modern imbalances: for example, reduced gastrointestinal activity leads to decreased nutrient absorption and irregular bowel movements; increased stress hormones that aren't properly eliminated by exercise or detoxification lead to mood swings, adrenal fatigue and insomnia; blood vessels are constricted, causing an increase in blood pressure and a faster heartbeat. Barefoot walking can bring these imbalances back into harmony, and help regulate our natural day/night cortisol rhythm. We sleep better, feel better and strengthen our natural resources.

It is also a simple way to bring ourselves back to the present, away from the whirrings of the mind and in towards the senses. Focus on your breath, the sensation of it entering as you inhale, and the warmth leaving your nostrils as you exhale. Turn your attention to the noises of nature surrounding you, both near and far away, and to the texture of the ground underneath your feet. Connect with each toe, each heel, each pore of your foot that is communing with the earth and absorbing its life force; let nature root you in the here and now.

AROMATHERAPY

Aromatherapy is one of my favourite holistic resources because it is so uplifting and accessible, and the options for personal customisations are infinite. In daily life, wherever it may take me, I am always blown away by how quickly an inhalation of tea tree or chamomile essential oil can turn my day around, whether I'm crammed on the Underground or racing to another meeting. It is one of the most precious tools for supporting people with burnout, fatigue or emotional disharmony.

Essential oils have been used by man since as long ago as 3,000 BC and we have always explored the power of plants to alter our mood and senses. In naturopathy, gentle tools such as this are a great starting point for taking your wellness back into your own hands: blending your own oils, exploring the fragrances you feel drawn to and connecting to the plant and its properties all serve to empower and support us on the journey to optimal health.

There are various ways to use essential oils: in the bath, with a burner or vaporiser, in a base oil as a topical blend or for massage, or incorporated into homemade skincare, which I find particularly useful. No longer confined to the artificial fragrances used by cosmetic brands, we can customise our products according to preference and change them up just as easily. I am forever exploring new combinations and the added challenge of a husband to please keeps me on my aromatherapy toes. When applied topically to the skin, essential oils can be very strong; you only need small amounts to safely benefit from the aromas. The recommended guidelines are 0.25% dilution for children aged 6 months to 6 years, and 1–2% dilution for adults. As a rule, one drop of oil with one teaspoon of a carrier oil will give you roughly 1% dilution. Higher concentrations can be used for specific therapeutic uses but these are only guidelines: you should always check instructions for use with the manufacturer before applying your own.

Almond and jojoba are popular flavourless carrier oils and are generally affordable, while stronger oils such as olive, sesame, hazelnut and wheatgerm have more distinctive flavours.

A little note: although it is rare, if you experience any irritation or unwellness from essential oils, you should stop using them immediately and seek medical advice if symptoms do not improve. Always avoid contact with eyes and broken skin. It is not encouraged to use essential oils on the skin during the first few months of pregnancy; if you are (or may be) pregnant or breastfeeding you should always consult the supplier before using them.

BAY Soothes rheumatic pains, aching muscles and respiratory congestion; boosts circulation.

BERGAMOT Uplifting; helps reduce anxiety, tension and stress. Also has antiseptic properties.

CARDAMOM Calming and soothing. Also helps digestion, nausea and respiratory congestion.

CHAMOMILE Promotes relaxation, harmony and has a sedative effect: one drop on the sole of each foot at night can help promote deep sleep. Also good for bee stings and rashes.

GERANIUM Uplifting, balancing and harmonising. Often used to balance oily or combination skin.

JASMINE Heady, uplifting, rejuvenating and relieves stress.

LAVENDER Calming and balancing. Also helpful for insomnia and regulating poor sleep patterns.

ORANGE Detoxifying, immunity-boosting and uplifting.

PEPPERMINT Cooling, refreshing and uplifting.

ROSE Energising and comforting – often used as an aphrodisiac.

SANDALWOOD Woody, grounding, relieves itching and has a mildly toning effect on the skin.

TEA TREE Antiseptic, antifungal, cooling and stimulating. Also good for clearing the sinuses.

The following blends use a combination of essential oils that work in harmony to address specific needs and moments.

EVERYDAY RELAXATION BLEND
Lavender, chamomile, bergamot

EVERYDAY UPLIFTING BLEND
Rose, geranium, lavender

WARMING BLEND
Cardamom, orange, sandalwood

TRAVEL BLEND
Lavender, peppermint, lemon, bergamot, bay

UNPLUGGING: A DIGITAL DETOX

In the modern age nothing threatens our wellbeing so incessantly as the round-the-clock call of technology. Although one of our greatest inventions and resources, it nonetheless places high demands on our vitality, and embarking on a regular digital detox, or 'unplugging', is essential for a balanced and mindful life.

Modern screens are particularly disruptive to our overall wellness as they interrupt our melatonin cycle: they produce the same blue light as the sun, which is a natural signal to our bodies to stop producing the sleep-inducing hormone so that we can wake up and emerge into the day. (Modern light bulbs emit the same blue light.) The result is that as we lie in bed checking our phones and computers, we struggle to attain deep sleep, and our 24/7 connectedness causes long-term insomnia and sleep disruption and prevents the body from the healing processes it usually performs at night. When our bodies are receiving conflicting messages regarding the time of day, our natural energy patterns, relaxation impulses and instinctive creativity are under increasing attack.

It isn't always easy – or possible – to abandon the screen completely for as long as we would like, but these three steps can help us return to a more natural cycle, and better focus on the tasks in hand when we do return to the screen.

A TECHNOLOGY-FREE BEDROOM

So many of us take our mobile phones and devices to bed and, with a screen being the last thing we see before sleeping and the first thing we encounter upon waking, there is little escape. Creating a technology-free sanctuary in the bedroom allows us to drop down into a calmer, simpler, more relaxed space where we can end and begin each day with reflection and intention as opposed to reacting to emails or passively scrolling through social media. A radio or conventional alarm clock is all you need by your bed; failing these, putting your phone in flight mode is a step in the right direction.

LIMITED BLUE LIGHT

Welcoming the evening with candlelight instead of electric bulbs can have an amazing effect on your nervous system and overall sense of wellbeing. Even if you just substitute one or two lights each evening, the transition creates a much more calming atmosphere that helps us switch off from the communications of the day, and turn inwards to reflect and process them.

UNPLUG ONE DAY A WEEK

If you can, encourage yourself or your household to unplug from all technology for one whole day a week. It is a powerful exercise in returning to basics and communing with your surroundings in a more integrated way and, with a little planning, not that difficult. Television, phones, email, social media – taking a break from these demands on our energy creates time and space for more basic human needs: walking in nature, communicating face to face, creative pursuits and physical exercise. It's a simple way to reset body and soul and realign with a life before technology.

MINDFUL LIVING

MINDFUL LIVING

INDEX

INDEX

INDEX

INDEX

BIOGRAPHY

Xochi's first career was as a trends journalist and freelance writer for the *Financial Times* and the *Evening Standard* before abandoning office life to set up a street food van, Rainbo. But with that life came long hours, unhealthy food and mounting stress, and a dawning realisation that she could not sustain this pace of life in the long term. Xochi enrolled at the College of Naturopathic Medicine and started writing The Naturalista blog as a means of documenting her journey back to vitality through food, natural beauty and mindfulness.

With her husband Ben, Xochi travels to various teachers and workshops in the UK and beyond to delve ever deeper into what it means to live a healthy, balanced and spiritually connected life.

www.thenaturalista.co.uk
@xochibalfour

ACKNOWLEDGEMENTS

Thank you to my mama: the most capable, efficient and stylish cook I know. Surely no Aga in the world has ever seen such glamour as yours. Thank you to my mother-in-law, Julia, your inimitable Sunday lunches have become the highlight of my calendar and you continually show me the importance, and joy, of making everything from scratch. Thank you to my sisters, who have always supported me in all my endeavours: Willa, your wisdom over the years has been invaluable; Kinvara, your unfailing support and honesty have kept me pushing forwards through the toughest times; and Jubie, I don't know how I will ever repay your patience when I was a useless waitress for you and ate all the canapés; your brilliant cooking and colourful vision are truly an inspiration. Thank you to my father, for always showering me in love and snuggles, and my father-in-law, Nigel, for your encouragement and generosity. Granny, you are an unthinkably talented maker of things and I hope I do you proud in the kitchen and beyond.

Diana, my brilliant agent, and Muna, my wonderful publisher — you made all this happen: eternal thanks for that. Thank you, Laura, for your patient support and editorial guidance; and Clare for keeping me on my grammatical toes!

Rahel, Charlotte, Jemima and Aya — you have been the dream team and your vision has been so inspiring. A thousand thank yous for all your dedication and energy in bringing these pages to life.

Lara and Seth — huge gratitude for so generously letting us scamper round 42 Acres for the perfect shots, and thank you also to Mike and Teasle for your endless generosity, inimitable style and constant support.

Alice — your patience as a best friend is worthy of a gold medal.

To our Pachamama family — mil gracias por todo. This is where it all began.

To Ben — my partner in so many adventures, the wind beneath my wings, thank you for teaching me to cook, treading this path with me, and showing me there is more to life than pasta, butter and cheese.

And to all of you who read my blog and have supported The Naturalista along the way, eternal thanks to each and every one of you.

First published in 2016
by HEADLINE PUBLISHING GROUP

1

Cataloguing in Publication Data is available from the British Library

Hardback ISBN 9781472232441

Art Direction and design: Charlotte Heal Design
Photography: Rahel Weiss
Project Editor: Laura Herring
Copy Editor: Clare Sayer
Food Stylist: Aya Nishimura
Props Stylist: Jemima Hetherington

Repro by the Born Group
Printed and bound in Germany by Mohn Media

Headline's policy is to use papers that are natural, renewable and recyclable
products and made from wood grown in sustainable forests. The logging and
manufacturing processes are expected to conform to the environmental regulations
of the country of origin.

HEADLINE PUBLISHING GROUP
An Hachette UK Company
Carmelite House
50 Victoria Embankment
London EC4 0DZ

www.headline.co.uk
www.hachette.co.uk